Nevada County
·WINE·

Nevada County
· W I N E ·

MARY ANNE DAVIS

AMERICAN PALATE

Published by American Palate
A Division of The History Press
Charleston, SC
www.historypress.com

Front cover: Mike Naggiar in Naggiar Vineyards. *Author photograph.*
Grapevines. *Author photograph.*
Bottles of wine courtesy of Nevada City Winery.
Lower photo courtesy of Naggiar Vineyards and Winery.

Back cover courtesy of the Union Newspaper.

First published 2020

Manufactured in the United States

ISBN 9781467139540

Library of Congress Control Number: 2019956046

Notice: The information in this book is true and complete to the best of our knowledge. It is offered without guarantee on the part of the author or The History Press. The author and The History Press disclaim all liability in connection with the use of this book.

To my granddaughter, Leah, for being my inspiration every day. You are a special young lady, and I hope you know that you can do anything you want with your life—the sky's the limit! I will love you forever and always.

Contents

CONTENTS

Acknowledgements

There are many people I need to thank for helping me write this book. First, I would like to thank my editor, Laurie Krill, who did not give up on me even when I said "no" to this book project. I said "no" two or three times before she convinced me that I could really do this.

I also want to thank my husband, Scott, who never complained that I'd come home from work and start researching and writing. Often, that meant that I couldn't prepare dinner or keep the house as clean as it could have been…he and our son, Andrew, fended for themselves so that I could work on this book. Scott was also my biggest fan and critic when I asked him for honest assessments of my writing. He's not a writer, but he is a voracious reader (averaging three to four books a week).

I would also like to thank my dear friend Chris Enss, an excellent and prolific author, for her encouragement, inspiration, friendship and advice throughout this experience. If I can someday be half the writer she is, I will feel very accomplished.

I also want to thank my friends who understood why I wasn't always as available to go out and have some fun—I had a strict schedule to keep in order to finish this book on time.

Then, of course, there are the lovely ladies of the Nevada County Historic Searls Library: Pat Chesnut, Linda Jack and Brita Rozynski. When I came looking for information and photos, they made finding what I needed so easy! They are truly the gold of our community, with their in-depth knowledge of the region's history.

ACKNOWLEDGEMENTS

I also want to thank the *Union Newspaper* in Grass Valley for allowing me to access their recorded history and historical photos that I needed for this endeavor. It is a community treasure.

My special thanks go to the local winery owners and managers who answered my questions and dug through photographs to help me find what I needed for this book.

I also want to say thank you to my wonderful parents, who were always my biggest fans and loved me unconditionally. I hope they're watching from heaven and are still proud of me. I miss them both every day.

I want to say one more heartfelt thank you to my husband of thirty-seven years, Scott Davis. His unwavering support of me when I want to jump in and try new things—like writing my first book—makes those experiences a lot less scary.

Introduction

The stories that happen around a bottle of wine are every bit as fascinating
if not more so than what's inside the bottle.
—Rod Byers, certified wine educator

Nevada County is rich in history—perhaps more so than most other areas in California. What seemed to define California, and especially western Nevada County, in the mid-1800s was the gold rush. The center of all of the profitable gold mining in California was in Grass Valley. Perhaps that's why that area is often referred to as "Gold Country." Many gold mines existed there, and as time went on, these mines were combined to create two of the largest mines in California: the Empire Mine and the North Star Mine. The Empire Mine was so well known and productive that the Smithsonian in Washington, D.C., has one of its rather large gold nuggets on display.

The liquid gold of the area has always been wine. Starting back as far as the gold rush, vineyards were planted and wine was produced in Grass Valley. The local wine industry had a lot of ups and downs; some years were very good, and some were quite bad. While none of the original vineyards that were planted in the 1800s still exist, the area has managed to rise again after each downturn.

This book is an outline of Nevada County's history in the wine industry, but to only tell this part of the county's story would not do it justice. There are many other momentous achievements and historical tidbits buried in Nevada County's past, including the gold rush, which gave the wine industry its texture and context. Wine grapes were not grown in a vacuum; Nevada County's history has been so interlaced with those of local vineyards and wine production that they all have to be told in order to be understood and appreciated.

On these pages, readers will learn about the history of the gold rush and some of Nevada County's other interesting moments, and they will learn how everything is interwoven into the history of the vineyards. The area's vineyards have come and gone (and come and gone again), but their stories ultimately led to the thirteen thriving wineries in the area today. It's the combination of Nevada County's history, natural beauty and wineries that make it a unique tourist destination for some and a very special home to others.

While there is no way for a single book to cover all of the area's history—or all of its details—this book is meant to whet its readers' appetites and encourage them to research their own interests. Nevada County has excellent museums, historical libraries and long-time residents that are all eager to tell their stories. Of course, Nevada County also has a number of wonderful wineries, with their own histories and stories that are told toward the end of this book. This book's intent is not to recommend one winery over another or to judge each winery on the quality of its wines; instead, it presents them all, in no particular order, as each one is unique and worthy of a visit.

The California Gold Rush (1848–55) had a major effect on the geography, economy and history of California's wine production. The gold rush also brought a large influx of people to Northern California—mainly to San Francisco (the city's population grew from 1,000 to 25,000 between January 1848 and December 1849). This increase in California's population caused a significant increase in the demand for wine and spurred an increase in wine production in the areas that were within one hundred miles of San Francisco.

The 1850s saw the expansion of wine production into many parts of Northern California, including Nevada County.

1
The Towns of Nevada County

N evada County is a truly magnificent area in the Sierra Nevada Foothills; its beauty, charm and history are unmatched. From the breathtakingly rugged Sierra Nevada Mountains in eastern Nevada County to the riches in the gold mines and agricultural fields of western Nevada County, the area has an incredibly rich history. Its many museums, state parks, historic buildings and landmarks offer an intriguing glimpse into Northern California's fascinating past.

Nevada County was created in 1851, when portions from Yuba County, which was quite large at the time, were combined and annexed by the new county. The old county's boundary lines were changed, and the new county was named after the mining town of Nevada City. The city derived its name from the Sierra Nevada Mountains—Nevada is Spanish for "snowy" or "snow-covered." Nevada County is one of California's most scenic and historic regions. Located in the Sierra Nevada Foothills, the county comprises 978 square miles (16 square miles are water), and it is mostly rural, with a population that is just under 100,000. Full of pristine rivers, lakes and lovely forest land, the area was quite awe-inspiring to those who made the journey from the eastern states. When the first wagons crossed the Sierra Nevada Mountains, they cleared the way for the Truckee River route of the California Trail, which came through Nevada County. The site of the ill-fated Donner Party—along with portions of the first transcontinental railroad and the first transcontinental road for automobiles—is also located in Truckee.

Main Street in Grass Valley. *Watercolor painting by Nevada City artist Loana Beason.*

There are three incorporated cities in Nevada County: Grass Valley and Nevada City in the western half and Truckee in the eastern half. The county also contains the communities of Penn Valley, Rough and Ready, Washington, Chicago Park, Peardale, North San Juan and French Corral. However, of the almost 100,000 people who live in Nevada County, 65,000 live in the unincorporated areas; only the remaining 30,000 or so residents live within the city limits of Truckee, Nevada City and Grass Valley. There is also quite a steep elevation difference between the eastern and western halves of Nevada County; Penn Valley has an elevation of 1,400 feet, Grass Valley has an elevation of 2,100 feet, Nevada City has an elevation that is closer to 2,500 and Truckee has an elevation that is just over 5,800. To travel from Nevada City to Truckee, one must go over the Donner Summit, which has an elevation of 7,057 feet.

As one would expect, there are significant climate differences between these varied elevations. Like much of Northern California, the western half of Nevada County has a classic Mediterranean climate, with warm summers and rainy winters that can sometimes include snowfall in some of its foothill elevations. These conditions are absolutely ideal when it comes to producing excellent grapes that create wines of distinction. Truckee, on the other hand, is often the coldest town in the nation between June and October; and in the winter, it receives quite a bit of snow, which is not at all conducive to grape growing.

NEVADA CITY

Nevada City is a national landmark town. Dedicated in 1985, Nevada City was recognized in the National Register of Historic Places as "the largest and best preserved historical downtown district in California Gold Country." The marker dedicated to this recognition is located in Calanan Park, on the corner of Broad and Union Streets in downtown Nevada City.

The plaque reads:

NATIONAL REGISTER OF HISTORIC PLACES
Nevada City, "Queen City of the Northern Mines," became a town of
10,000 to 16,000 in the early 1850s following the discovery of gold
on Deer Creek in 1849. Here is located the largest and best preserved
historical downtown district in the California Gold Country. As the
county seat of Nevada County, Nevada City has maintained its position
as the county's center of government, professional services and cultural
activities since its beginning in 1851.
Entered National Register of Historic Places, September 23, 1985.
Native Sons of the Golden West. Hydraulic Parlor No. 56. Grand Parlor,
Robert Souza, Grand President
Funded by James D. Phelan Trust

In addition to all of the wonderful history in Nevada City, there are three wineries that call the city home: Nevada City Winery, Szabo Vineyards and Double Oak Vineyards and Winery.

GRASS VALLEY

The City of Grass Valley is the largest city in western Nevada County. It was originally known as Boston Ravine and, later, Centerville, but when the post office was established in 1851, the town was renamed Grass Valley. Rumor has it that the town was named by settlers whose cattle had wandered away from their campsite on Greenhorn Creek. They called it "grassy valley," because it was better grazing for cattle.[1]

Three of the largest and richest gold mines in California—the Empire Mine, the North Star Mine and the Idaho-Maryland Mine—are located in Grass Valley. At one time, around the 1890s, Grass Valley's population was about 75 percent Cornish; the tin miners of Cornwall, England, had skills that were needed to mine gold. The town still holds onto its Cornish heritage with Cornish Christmas celebrations and other traditions that are rooted in Cornish history. Downtown Grass Valley is only four miles west of downtown Nevada City, and over the years, the two cities have practically merged as they've expanded. It isn't always easy to tell where one town ends and the other begins.

Four wineries also call Grass Valley home: Sierra Starr Vineyard and Winery, Lucchesi Vineyards and Winery, Avanguardia Winery and Naggiar Vineyards.

"Grass Valley Gal, Looking West, 1889, Compliments of Nevada Co. N.G.R.R. Co." *Courtesy of Searls Historical Library PIC4-GR-72A.*

PENN VALLEY

Located just six miles west of Grass Valley is a town called Penn Valley. In addition to its beautiful scenery, Penn Valley is known for its vineyards, pastures, livestock, Heritage Oaks and the beautiful 88-acre Western Gateway Park. Penn Valley was named after Madame Penn, who, in the early 1800s, homesteaded 320 acres in the area where Squirrel and Grub Creeks intersect. In 1852, James Ennor, a gold miner turned rancher, purchased the property from Madame Penn. He continued to acquire land until the original 320 acres grew to 700 acres, which eventually became a large part of the modern town of Penn Valley.[2] This area was also home to the Maidu and Nisenan tribes, and they were followed by gold miners in 1848.

Penn Valley, which is thought to have been one of the first settlements in Nevada County, was also part of a major freight wagon route that served the mining regions in the east and Sacramento in the west. Penn Valley was an important stop along this route because of its livery and blacksmithing services. Penn Valley was also home to a thriving dairy industry, which

View of the expansive lawn leading down to the amphitheater at Western Gateway Park, Penn Valley. *Author photograph.*

Buttermaker's Cottage in Western Gateway Park, Penn Valley. *Courtesy of Nancy Peirce.*

included a creamery that was reported to be one of the best in California. The Buttermaker's Cottage in Western Gateway Park was once home to that creamery.

Since the Penn Valley area had rich soil and a warm climate, its leaders attempted to persuade would-be gold miners to be farmers and ranchers. As the gold miners became discouraged, many of them turned to agriculture and farming. This trend led to the area becoming known as the "Pantry of the Northern Mines"; Penn Valley provided fresh fruit, vegetables and meat for freight trains that were heading to mines in states as far away as Nevada.[3]

Today, Penn Valley is a thriving community that is somewhat split between two town centers: central Penn Valley and a gated residential community called Lake Wildwood. Two wineries are located near Penn Valley: Gray Pine Vineyard and Winery and Pilot Peak Winery.

FRENCH CORRAL

The little town of French Corral has a pretty big claim to fame; in 1877, the Ridge Telephone Company built the world's first long-distance telephone line in French Corral, which connected it to French Lake (now named Bowman Lake). This line started at the headwaters of the Yuba River and was strung across poles and trees for fifty-eight miles through Nevada County. The line passed through Birchville, Sweetland, North San Juan, Cherokee, North Columbia, Lake City, North Bloomfield, Moore's Flat, Graniteville and Milton. Thirty "Edison speaking instruments," or phones, were installed at stations along the route. This was the first use of long-distance telephone wires since the telephone's invention by Dr. Alexander G. Bell two years earlier. The mine operators in the region immediately saw the benefit of having instant communication; with it, they were able to control the flow of water along the miles of ditches that were used for hydraulic mining.[4]

This long-distance telephone line was operated by the Milton Mining Company from a building in French Corral that was constructed in 1853. In French Corral, there is a monument called California Historical Landmark 247 that states, "World's First Long Distance Telephone Line." It is located three miles east of the Bridgeport Covered Bridge.

ROUGH AND READY

The Great Republic of Rough and Ready, which is located between Grass Valley and Penn Valley, also has its own unique history. Rough and Ready seceded from the United States of America in April 1850, in order to avoid paying taxes on its mining claims.

The town of Rough and Ready elected Colonel E.F. Brundage as their president, and they drafted a constitution with which to govern their new country. This new country lasted until July 4, 1850 (for less than three months), when its citizens realized that they could no longer celebrate the Fourth of July. They quickly convened and, by a popular vote, decided to rejoin the United States of America.

Rough and Ready still celebrates "Secession Days" on the last Sunday in June to remember their short-lived status as the world's smallest nation.

A replica of an Old West town in Rough and Ready, which belongs to Dr. and Mrs. Jacobitz. The horse's name is Brady. *Author photograph.*

NORTH SAN JUAN

Not far from downtown Nevada City (about thirteen miles up California State Route 49) is a town called North San Juan. The town dates back to the California Gold Rush, when it began to prosper from the hydraulic mining that took place in nearby Malakoff Diggins State Historic Park from 1850 to 1884. In 1867, North San Juan was included on the route of the first long-distance telephone line that was stretched between French Corral and French Lake.

The town's original name, San Juan, was chosen by a Mexican-American War veteran who settled there in 1853 and thought that the land looked like San Juan de Ulua near Veracruz, Mexico. When the town's post office opened in 1857, the word "North" was added to keep people from confusing it with the town of San Juan in San Benito County.

The modern-day drive to North San Juan is beautiful, although the path through the river canyon can be winding. Today, the community isn't quite as booming as it was during the gold rush; it consists of a few businesses, organic farms and peaceful homes. While Double Oak Vineyards and Winery is technically in Nevada City, it is much closer to North San Juan.

CHICAGO PARK

Chicago Park (formerly Storms Station) is located about nine miles southeast of downtown Grass Valley on Highway 174. Historically, it was an agricultural and wine-growing community. Prior to the 1840s, this area was populated by the Nisenan, who are sometimes referred to as the Northern Maidu.

Chicago Park got its name from its founding residents, who were developers from Chicago, Illinois. In late 1887, they moved to the area to create the Chicago Park Colony, which consisted of twenty- and forty-acre parcels, a town square and a number of lots for businesses around the square. While most of the founders' plans were never realized, they were able to sell around seven thousand acres of land, mostly to Chicago residents. Some of these developers moved to Chicago Park to grow grapes, make wine and ship it back to Illinois for consumption.

Chicago Park's fruit industry was extremely prosperous; the area had a great number of orchards that grew pears, peaches, plums and apples. The railroad transported the fruit to distribution centers, and visitors can still see the 1930s Pacific Fruit Packing Shed at the intersection of Lower Colfax Road and Mount Olive Road. As one of California's first wine-grape-growing regions, Chicago Park is currently home to two local wineries: Montoliva Vineyard and Winery and Clavey Vineyards and Winery.

WASHINGTON

The small town of Washington, California, is nineteen miles outside Nevada City, just off of California State Route 20. Washington was originally named Indiana Camp by miners who had traveled to the region from Indiana in 1849. The town was renamed Washington in 1850. The town is located on the upper banks of the south fork of the Yuba River, which produced quite a bit of placer gold. The region was also home to a number of hard rock mines and hydraulic mines, and evidence of this remains today.

At an elevation of 3,652 feet, Washington is the only settlement in the area that has survived to the present day. During the gold rush, Washington had a large Chinese population. Today, only a few hundred people call Washington, California, home, and the town's population varies seasonally, with increased tourism in the summers.

TRUCKEE

Truckee, a High Sierra district in what is considered to be eastern Nevada County, offers world-class scenery and a rugged alpine location that inspires art and culture. Truckee's rich history includes the arrival of the Transcontinental Railroad (which celebrated its Sesquicentennial in 2019), the story of the infamous Donner Party, performances by Charlie Chaplin and the events of the 1960 Winter Olympics in nearby Squaw Valley. Some of the best skiing in the country can also be found at many of Truckee's nearby ski resorts. The majestic and powerful Truckee River flows right through Truckee's historic downtown district; the river is 121 miles long and flows between Lake Tahoe in California and Pyramid Lake in Nevada.

As a railroad town, Truckee was originally called Coburn Station in honor of the local saloon keeper. Truckee encompasses 33.7 square miles (1.3 square miles are water), including the Truckee River, the only outlet for Lake Tahoe. Truckee's Hilltop Lodge had one of the first mechanized ski lifts. The lodge is now the site of the Cottonwood Restaurant and Bar, which overlooks downtown Truckee and the Truckee River. In Truckee's historic downtown, visitors can find many outstanding art galleries and can participate in a number of workshops and events. Visitors can also see the Transcontinental Railroad, which once traveled right through downtown. The tracks are now used by people traveling across the country on Amtrak's passenger lines.

The Rex Hotel was built in the early 1900s and, in 1913, was converted to a hotel with steam-heated rooms. During Prohibition, the lower floor was a speakeasy called the Silver Mirror.[5] Another historic Truckee hotel, the American Hotel, was built in 1873; however, a fire destroyed a majority of the hotel's structure in 1909. The hotel has been through many name changes over the years, the most notable of which was its change to the

Truckee River near historic downtown Truckee. *Author photograph.*

The Hilltop Lodge was the site of Truckee's first mechanical ski lift. *Author photograph.*

Historic downtown Truckee. Notice the still-visible sign on the old Hotel Rex. Rooms cost just one dollar per night. *Author photograph.*

Alpine Riverside Hotel during the 1960 Winter Olympics at Squaw Valley. It was officially renamed the Truckee Hotel in 1977 after a major renovation.

Truckee's historic downtown area is also home to two very interesting museums: the Old Jail Museum and the Railroad Museum. The Old Jail was built in 1875; it was constructed using native stone (the current brick structures weren't added until 1904). Although prisons are typically built to be strong, Truckee's prison was much stronger than most. The original prison only comprised the lower level of the current building. Its walls were thirty-two inches thick; it had no windows and there were only small vents for each cell, which were enclosed with irregular rows of two-inch-thick steel bars. The ceilings were made from plate steel, insulated with dirt and lined with narrow gauge railroad tracks. All of the doors were made of riveted steel and weighed approximately two hundred pounds apiece. The jail ran continuously until it was closed in 1964, and during that time, it housed many infamous criminals.[6]

The first transcontinental railroad, the logging railroads and the passenger railroads all played an important part in Truckee's history. The Railroad Museum, which is located next to the depot and chamber of commerce

The Old Truckee Jail, built in 1875, was used up until 1964. It is now a museum. *Author photograph.*

in Truckee's historic downtown, is housed in a Southern Pacific Railroad caboose. Although the construction of the Sierra railway tunnels took longer than expected, advance teams began building forty miles of track on both the east and west sides of Truckee and moved the supplies they needed by wagon and sled. The line reached Truckee on April 3, 1868; construction continued east toward the Union Pacific line at the rate of one mile per day. On May 10, 1869, the rails met at Promontory, Utah, and completed the first transcontinental railroad. Truckee's depot was built in 1900 and is used today as an Amtrak depot.

History of Wine in California

W hen you look at the history of wine in California, its scope pales in comparison to the scope of the history of wine around the world. Some early pieces of archaeological evidence of wine produced from grapes have been found at sites in China (7000 BC), Georgia (the country, not the state) (6000 BC), Iran (5000 BC), Greece (4500 BC) and Sicily (4000 BC). The earliest evidence of wine production was found in Armenia (4100 BC). American wine has been produced for over three hundred years; today, wine is produced in all fifty states, with California producing 89 percent of all the wine in the United States.[7] Overall, the United States is the fourth-largest wine-producing country in the world, after Italy, Spain and France.[8]

The history of wine in California begins with the arrival of the Spanish. The first vineyards in the state were planted by the Spanish Franciscan missionaries at California's first mission, Mission San Diego de Alcalá, in 1769. Just as the missionaries had planted palm trees to produce palm leaves for Palm Sunday, they planted vineyards to make the sacramental wine for communion. The first variety of grapes that were planted by Father Junípero Serra became so pervasive that they became known as Mission grapes (also known as Listan Prieto), and they dominated commercial viticulture in California until the 1880s.[9] In 1833, the first documented European vines were planted in Los Angeles by Jean-Louis Vignes, the state's first commercial winemaker. It wasn't until the gold rush that vines were planted in Northern California, in Nevada, Napa and Sonoma Counties.[10]

As an interesting side note, Missouri also played a significant role in the history of wine in America. In the 1870s, a German immigrant named George Husmann—and other Missourian grape growers—shipped millions of American grape cuttings to France and other European countries so that they could save vineyards that had been infected with the insect phylloxera.[11] Using phylloxera-free cuttings and rootstock was the best way for the Europeans to fight the pests. Husmann, the founder of Hermannhof Winery, is known as the father of the Missouri wine industry. Most are surprised to hear that Missouri was the nation's second-largest wine producer before Prohibition (New York was the largest).

1852: THE FIRST VINEYARDS IN NEVADA COUNTY

At this point in history, clean, safe drinking water was not readily available. People relied on alcohol, because it typically did not make them sick (unless, of course, they over-imbibed); it was often safer to drink alcohol. Wine has been made and sold in Grass Valley since French and Italian immigrants settled there in the mid-1800s. One of the first wineries in the county was the Personeni Winery on Jones Bar Road; it was less than a mile from present-day Avanguardia Winery, which is five miles west of Nevada City.

During the gold rush, San Francisco was the port of entry for tens of thousands of people who were heading east to the gold fields. There were no bridges then, so people had to take the southern route, around the bay, and pass through places like Mission San Jose. Friars had planted grapes at all twenty-one of the California missions; each mission was centered around its grapes and wine that was made from its grapes. While visiting the missions, the miners took cuttings of the Mission grape vines and brought them along on their journeys.[12] Another popular stop along the road to the gold mines was Smith's Pomological Gardens, which was located on the American River in the Sacramento area. The miners often collected Zinfandel grape cuttings from the gardens to add to their collection. Mission and Zinfandel grapes eventually became the two most prevalent grape varieties grown in Nevada County vineyards.[13]

In 1862, Mr. Isoarde, a Nevada City saloon owner, served wines that were produced with local grapes at his Broad Street saloon.[14] In 1866, the county assessor reported that 124,000 vines and 10,000 gallons of wine had been produced. It is suspected that this estimate was low because of a

Vineyard in Nevada County. *Watercolor painting by Nevada City artist Loana Beason.*

tax that had been imposed on production of wine. Some wineries may not have fully reported their production rates in order to save money on taxes; the actual amount may have been at least twice the estimated number (or 20,000 gallons).

At that time, grapes were grown in Grass Valley, Nevada City, North San Juan, French Corral, Chicago Park and Rough and Ready. All of these towns had slightly different elevations and microclimates, which produced a nice variety of wines. By 1870, there were several hundred acres of vineyards, with 450,000 vines, in western Nevada County. At that time, some California wines were being sold for two dollars per gallon, which was quite a good price at the time.[15] In 1869, Frank Siebert of Nevada City produced a Zinfandel that was one of the first to win a medal in a California wine competition.[16] Mr. Edwin G. Waite, a newspaperman in Nevada City, produced a wine that was considered to be as good as French Clarets. California wine was at its peak.

As the 1870s continued, the landscape of California's wine industry changed once again. The financial depression after the Civil War impacted many of America's economic industries, including California's wine industry. Nevada County suddenly had a surplus of grapes, which was mostly due to the fact that the grapes in California's Central Valley were cheaper. In 1871, Nevada County's seven distilleries produced a record four thousand gallons of brandy from local grapes; however, four times that number of grapes went unpicked and rotted in the vineyards. The local wineries couldn't sell all the wine that they had produced, and the industry was floundering. It was around this time that the original Nevada City Winery emerged as a wine cooperative with the goal of helping California growers through difficult times.

But just as there are peaks and valleys in Northern California's geographical landscape, there are also ups and downs in the area's economy; the downturn of the 1870s was followed by a boom in wine production in the 1880s. As the economy recovered, the demand for wine again increased. It didn't hurt that planting vineyards once again became the thing to do for gentlemen farmers. During this time, Mr. Edwin Waite of the *Nevada Journal* made the statement that, someday, Nevada County's wine would become "more valuable than gold."[17] In 1887, over two hundred acres of grapes were being grown by seventeen different vineyards. Of those seventeen vineyards, ten of them were also producing their own wine. In 1889, Nevada City Winery produced eight thousand gallons of wine.

Just when things were looking good for Nevada County's wineries and vineyards, the economy took yet another downturn. With the 1890s came a severe national depression. Money was tight, and nobody wanted to buy anything that they didn't need—luxuries were no longer purchased, and in those days, wine was considered a luxury. At the same time, the residents of Nevada County were planting vineyards and building wineries. The residents of Sonoma, Napa, Santa Clara and San Jose were also busy building their wine industries. When California emerged from the depression of the 1890s, the state's financiers preferred to invest their money in industries that were closer to home and San Francisco. However, Nevada County and the Sierra Foothills were just too far away for investors to risk putting their money into those wineries.

By the time Prohibition was repealed in 1933, the once-thriving wine industry in the United States had nearly been destroyed. Between 1919 and 1925, the nation's wine production had dropped by 94 percent. Before 1920, there were over 2,500 commercial wineries in the United States, but by the end of Prohibition, less than 100 remained. The University of California, Davis (UC–Davis) started offering viticulture and enology programs in an effort to revitalize the wine industry. Maynard Amerine was one of the first faculty members to be hired into this new program. Even with the help of the wine-making experts at UC–Davis and Maynard Amerine's writing, traveling and advising, the wine industry's turnaround was slow. By 1960, the number of wineries in the United States had only grown from about 100 to 271. It would take more than a half-century for winemaking in California to return to its pre-Prohibition levels.[18]

The small group of winemakers that resided in Northern California dedicated themselves to creating a winemaking industry that could compete internationally. But even after they began making high-quality wines, California's winemakers had a difficult time marketing their wines to consumers. The state's large-scale wineries, like Gallo, were selling large quantities of wine at low rates, and people became used to that level of quality and pricing.

The turning point for California wine occurred on May 24, 1976, when California's wine producers entered their wines in a blind tasting in France. The tasting was organized by British wine expert Steven Spurrier, and the panel of judges was exclusively French, so it was a shock when California's wines were ranked highest in both of the competitive categories.[19] A 1973 Chardonnay by Miljenko "Mike" Grgich at Chateau Montelena Winery took first place in the chardonnay category, and a 1973 Stag's Leap Wine Cellars cabernet sauvignon won first place in the reds category. The results of what came to be known as the "Judgment of Paris" were reported in multiple news outlets, including *Time Magazine*—California just couldn't buy press like that. The demand for California wines surged, and today, the state is recognized for creating some of the best wines in the world. Those competitive wines are still being produced today.

3

Before the Gold Rush: The Nisenan

P rior to the gold rush of 1848, approximately four thousand Maidu and Nisenan tribal members inhabited the land around Nevada County. The Nisenan had lived there for thousands of years before the gold rush, and they lived as a part of a perfectly balanced ecosystem, which thrived off of the Yuba, American and Bear Rivers.[20]

The Nisenan are a group of Native Americans and an indigenous people of California who lived along the watersheds of the Yuba and American Rivers in Northern California and the California Central Valley. The Nisenan people originally came from a larger group of Native American people known as the Maidu. The Nisenan people are now considered to be a part of the Northern Maidu.

A view of the shacks at Campoodie in Nevada City circa 1907. *Courtesy of M. Rieder, California Historical Society Collection at University of Southern California.*

THE NISENAN AND THE GOLD RUSH

The Nisenan were initially not affected by the cultural influences of European-American immigrants, and their initial meetings with Spanish and American expeditions in the early 1800s were peaceful. In 1833, a severe malaria epidemic struck the native population, which killed many Nisenan and a great number of neighboring tribal members.[21] The 1849 Gold Rush led to the appropriation and decimation of their land and brought an influx of disease, violence and mass murder. The Nisenan were a peaceful people, but they were treated like outcasts (and worse) on their own land—life as they knew it was over.[22] The influx of European immigrants during the gold rush (and their excessive use and abuse of the land) put a strain on the environment; eventually, this strain prompted a drought, and starvation took over. The Nisenan Maidu population dropped from approximately 9,000 to 2,500 by 1895, and only a fraction of the surviving Nisenan remained in the Sierra Nevada foothills.[23] In Brooke Schueller and Avery White's article "The California Tribe the Government Tried to Erase in the '60s" they said, "Some tribal elders estimate that, in the 1850s, there were 7,000 Nisenan Native Americans living in what is now considered Nevada City, California. According to the official tribal rolls, only 147 Nisenan live here today."[24]

While gold rush history seems to dominate the area, the story of the Nisenan people is a story that remains to be told—and it needs to be told. In simple terms, their history is marked by pain and oppression, which was caused by many of those who came in search of gold. "We had an entire society that was here thousands of years before the gold rush," said Shelly Covert, the tribal council secretary of the local Nisenan Tribe. "I've been trying to raise our tribe's visibility, but it's really tough."

Exterior view of Dudrais, which was used by the Nisenan, circa 1907.
Courtesy of California Historical Society Collection at University of Southern California.

The U.S. government officially recognizes 562 Native American tribes. This recognition provides federal protection for native lands and gives those tribes access to financial support. Unfortunately, the Nisenan tribe is not included in the list of recognized tribes, so it doesn't receive the protections it needs. The lack of recognition of the Nisenan is mainly due to the liquidation of the rancheria system in California; this system initially granted tracts of land to Native American tribes and offered federal support. The Rancheria Act of 1958 terminated 41 California rancherias, and the Nisenan was one of them. Currently, there are efforts being made to reverse the Rancheria Act and to, once again, get the Nisenan federally recognized. The remaining Nisenan are also working to rebuild and restore their sacred places and to preserve, share and cherish their history—they want to keep their culture alive.

4

Solid Gold

M uch of California's history revolves around the gold rush, which began in 1848. Nevada County exists, in large part, because of the leading role it played in the gold rush. In fact, the beginnings of the local wine industry are directly tied to the gold rush, as some of the first grapevines were brought to the region by gold miners.

California's gold was first discovered by James W. Marshall in 1848 at Sutter's Mill in Coloma, which is located south of the Grass Valley area. Once the gold was proven to be real (there was some initial doubt), word of its discovery spread quickly. It wasn't long before more than 300,000 people flocked to Northern California from all around the world to find their fortune in gold. The times were changing quickly, and these changes were accompanied by a lot of turmoil.

Placer gold was first found locally in Wolf Creek, which is located in what came to be called Grass Valley, in 1848. This discovery came shortly after Marshall's encounter with gold at Sutter's Mill. The gold in Wolf Creek was discovered by three gentlemen who had traveled there from Oregon. The placer gold quickly ran out in this particular location, and the men moved on. It wasn't until October 1850, when gold-bearing quartz was found on Gold Hill by George Knight (or George McKnight), that the area became viable for gold mining.[25]

GOLD QUARTZ DISCOVERY SITE ON "GOLD HILL"

George Knight was the man who first discovered gold on Gold Hill in Grass Valley (at that time, it was known as Boston Ravine) in October 1850. After this discovery, Gold Hill became the first site of quartz gold mining in the area. The Gold Hill Mine produced $4 million in gold between 1850 and 1857. At that time, gold was sold for about $21 per ounce, so it took approximately 190,476 ounces of gold for the Gold Hill Mine to achieve $4 million in profit.[26] At today's prices (at the time of this book's publication date, gold was sold at $1,550 per ounce) the gold produced by the Gold Hill Mine would be worth approximately $295 million. The marker below can be found on the corner of Jenkins Street and Hocking Avenue, just a few blocks from Condon Park in Grass Valley.

The monument on Gold Hill that commemorates George Knight's discovery of gold in October 1850. *Author photograph.*

GOLD MINING METHODS

Most people are familiar with gold panning, a placer mining method that used a gold pan to sift through soil and find gold in streams and riverbeds. After scooping up some soil and swirling it around for a bit, the heavier materials would sink to the bottom of the pan; miners hoped to find gold at the bottom, as it is heavier than sand and other rocks. It wasn't very effective, especially since miners wanted to sift through a lot of dirt and sediment quickly, so many prospectors only used gold panning until better methods were developed. Eventually, sluice boxes and dredges were developed, and they were able to wash through sediment a bit faster than gold pans.

NEW MINING METHODS

In 1850, traditional placer-mining methods, which used water to wash gold deposits from the sand and gravel of stream beds, became ineffective in this area; instead, miners turned to "hard rock" methods for mining gold. Hard rock methods involved miners lowering themselves into deep shafts (that were also known as coyote holes and resembled water wells) in buckets. Once underground, miners chipped and drilled holes through the rock, filled them with black powder (or dynamite) and detonated them. The resulting explosions created smaller pieces of rock, which were then loaded onto ore cars and taken to the mines' headframes for primary crushing. The miners who scooped up the blasted rock were called "muckers" and were considered entry-level employees at the gold mines.

After the ore was processed through primary crushing, it was taken to the stamp mills, where it was crushed into even smaller pieces. Stamp mills were comprised of a set of heavy steel (or sometimes iron-covered wood) stamps, which were loosely held in vertical frames so the stamps could slide up and down. The stamps were lifted by cams on horizontal rotating shafts, and each stamp fell onto the ore below, crushing the rock; this process was repeated continuously. Those who lived in the region could hear the stamp mills working from all over town, during all hours. At the stamp mill, the crushed ore was mixed with water and placed on copper plates that were coated with mercury. The mercury-coated copper combined with the "free" gold to form an amalgam. Water was

The stamp mill that was used by the Empire Mine. *Author photograph.*

used to wash away the contaminants before the amalgam was sent to the refinery for further processing.

Mining, especially hydraulic mining (a placer mining method in which high-powered water cannons were used to wash away rock and sediment), caused a high amount of environmental harm to the area. Evidence of the damage can still be seen in several locations, including the backside of Cascade Shores near Lost Mine Lake. Perhaps the largest of the hydraulic mining scars can be seen at Malakoff Diggins.

MALAKOFF DIGGINS STATE HISTORIC PARK

Located on 3,143 acres, just 26 miles outside of Nevada City, is a state historic park called Malakoff Diggins. This park was the site of a gold discovery in 1851, and it contains the most blatant example of hydraulic mining damage. These 3,143 acres contain 22 miles of trails, 30 campsites, 3 rustic miners' cabins, group campsites and several picnic sites. It is one of the best-preserved ghost towns in the West, as the once-thriving town of North Bloomfield (which at one time had a population of 2,000) is completely contained within the state park. The Malakoff Diggins State Historic Park was established in 1965, and it serves as a reminder of the complex and profound effects that gold mining had on the landscape of the region.[27]

Hydraulic mining, a gold extraction method that used high-pressure water (seven water cannons were used in this location) to wash away gold-bearing gravel, became popular in 1853. It was used until 1884, when it was outlawed due to the significant destruction it caused to the land. Although the technique was efficient in removing the layers of rock and earth that covered the gold-bearing gravel, the highly pressurized water that was used to move 41 million cubic yards of earth in this area left an open pit that is over a mile long and 600 feet deep. Today, the stark, scarred walls of the pit stand as a reminder of how destructive hydraulic mining was to the community.[28] In addition to the area's ravaged hillsides, the hydraulic mine tailings that washed away clogged the area's rivers and streams, flooded the valley floor and destroyed farmlands. The 1884 Sawyer Decision imposed much-needed restrictions on the disposal of hydraulic debris into the waterways.[29]

Today, visitors can see the dig sites and restored gold rush village of North Bloomfield at the park's center. The town contains a museum, the Ostrom Livery and Stable, the Smith-Knotwell Drugstore, the Kings Saloon, the Masonic Hall, the McKillican and Mobley General Store, a restored church, a blacksmith shop and a schoolhouse. Add these to several mining exhibits and a summertime guided history walk and you have a fascinating outing.

By the mid-1850s, an estimated 120,000 miners were living in California. Mining for gold was hard and dirty work. The price of living this lifestyle was high, and living conditions were bad. Only a few miners ever really struck it rich—most miners' profits ended up in the pockets of merchants and suppliers who offered products and services that the miners needed,

Top: The damage that was caused by years of hydraulic mining remains at Malakoff Diggins Historic State Park. *Courtesy of Katie Miller.*

Bottom: The old drugstore in Malakoff Diggins Historic State Park. *Courtesy of Katie Miller.*

like boarding, liquor, food and clothing. By 1873, the number of miners in California had dropped to about 30,000.[30] Gold mining had become more of a business and less of an adventure. Normally, the only people who actually became wealthy from gold mining were the mines' owners, like William Bourn of the Empire Mine, who built large hard rock and hydraulic mines that provided jobs to hundreds of men.

The rich underground mines in Grass Valley made that area the richest mining community in all of California. In fact, during the Great Depression of the 1930s, this area thrived on its gold mining–based economy. Truly, no depression was felt there. Author Gage McKinney even wrote a book titled *The 1930s: No Depression Here*; it tells the amazing story of how gold from the richest mining districts in California made boom towns in Nevada City and Grass Valley while the rest of America suffered unemployment and financial collapse during the Great Depression. Northern California's population doubled between 1930 and 1940, and the people there had jobs that paid living wages. Families were able to buy houses and cars, which further boosted the local economy.

There are some very interesting gold rush artifacts on display around the region, and they are worth seeing. A trip to observe these artifacts would further illustrate this book's history of Nevada County.

OTT'S ASSAY OFFICE

In the 1800s, assay offices were used to receive gold and silver bullion deposits from the public; these offices would then test the purity of the precious metals to ensure that no phony metals were being passed off as pure. Once the metal was tested, assay offices typically stamped a hallmark on the item to certify that its metallurgical content had passed inspection.[31]

Ott's assay office in Nevada City. *Author photograph.*

Assayer James J. Ott, cousin of John Sutter, who was in Nevada City from 1852 to 1859. *Courtesy of California Historical Society Collection at University of Southern California.*

James J. Ott was one of the best metallurgists in the West. For one hundred years, the Ott family played an important role in developing the gold and silver industries of California and Nevada. In 1859, the work of James J. Ott led to the discovery of the famous Comstock Lode in the state of Nevada. The building that housed Ott's assay office is both a national and Nevada County landmark, and it is located at the foot of Main Street in Nevada City.

PELTON WHEEL AND FIRE STAMP MILL

The Fire Stamp Mill was built in 1893 to crush ore at the Fortuna Mine. This particular Pelton wheel was used in Pacific Gas and Electric's drum division from 1928 to 1987. Pacific Gas & Electric (PG&E) donated these pieces of history to Nevada City in 1987. They are now located at the foot of Commercial Street, near the Nevada City Chamber of Commerce office and the site of Ott's assay office.[32]

CALANAN PARK MONITOR AND DRILL CORE

In 1853, the first hydraulic mine was built on American Hill, just outside of Nevada City. This large water cannon, which was called a monitor, used pressurized water to wash away the dirt that was covering gold-bearing

Stamp mill and Pelton wheel display in Robinson Plaza, Nevada City. *Author photograph.*

Water monitor that was used for hydraulic mining in Calanan Park, Nevada City. *Author photograph.*

Calanan Park mining history display. The cylindrical stone is a mining core. *Author photograph.*

gravel beds. Hydraulic mining was a profitable, yet destructive, way to mine, and it was used until 1884, when the Sawyer Decision outlawed it.

The shaft drill core in Calanan Park is used to represent hard rock mining. This particular core came from Grass Valley's Idaho-Maryland Mine, around the 1930s. (The mine itself was built in the 1860s.) Both the water monitor and the shaft drill core are located at the foot of Broad Street in downtown Nevada City.

GOLD RUSH STONEMASONS

Mining camps were normally filled with clusters of tents and other makeshift shelters, because until miners started to mine, they never knew whether a site would produce enough gold or not. If a mine was found to be productive enough, wooden buildings would be built to create a small mining town. Unfortunately, these mining towns were often destroyed by fire; the wood was extremely flammable, and there were no efficient or effective ways to fight fires at the time.

Above: The Kohler Building in Washington, California. *Courtesy of the California Historical Society Collection at University of Southern California.*

Right: 1853 Wells Fargo and Co. building in French Corral. *Courtesy of Elias Funez.*

In an effort to curtail this kind of devastation, stonemasons began building "fireproof" banks and stores out of bricks and stones. The addition of iron doors and shutters helped further protect these structures from burning down. Several of these stone buildings are still standing in Nevada County.[33] They include:

The Kohler Building was built in 1861 by Henry Kohler, a pioneer merchant and German-born miner who came to Washington from Indiana when he was twenty-nine years old. He mined until 1861, when he opened a general store that sold supplies, groceries and hardware. It is speculated that Henry made more money as a store owner than he did as a miner.[34]

The Nevada Theatre, which was built in 1865 in downtown Nevada City, is California Historical Landmark No. 863. This theater is thought to be the oldest original theater that still functions as a theater in California. Lola Montez, Lotta Crabtree, Emma Nevada and Mark Twain were all reported to have performed there. To this day, many local theater groups and organizations perform in the Nevada Theatre.

The Wells Fargo branch in French Corral, which was built in 1853, is a beautiful building that is situated on Pleasant Valley Road, about four-and-a-half miles west of Highway 49 and three miles east of the Bridgeport

Covered Bridge. French Corral, which was named for a stock pen that belonged to a French settler, was built as a mining town in 1849 after placer gold was discovered nearby.

The North San Juan Wells Fargo was built in 1854 as an office space and a holding center for currency and gold. From 1861 to 1869, the building was home to the Block and Furth Clothing Store. The building later housed a Chinese laundromat and store that was operated by Happy Go Lucky from 1890 to 1920. Since 1934, the building has been home to a bar and liquor store that was first owned by a woman named "Ma" Cunningham.

THE NEVADA BREWERY

Built in 1850, the Nevada Brewery's building was lost in a fire in 1856; it was then rebuilt by George Cehrig. He hired Italian stonemasons and Chinese laborers to rebuild the brewery from locally quarried blocks of granite, and they built the structure one stone at a time. The building is currently the site of the Stone House Restaurant, near the corner of Boulder Street and Sacramento Street in Nevada City.

Originally the Nevada Brewery in 1857, this building is now the Stone House Restaurant. *Author photograph.*

A storage cave was also dug alongside the brewery and was used as a place to age casks of ale. The cave was once connected to a network of tunnels that ran underneath Nevada City, but most of them were filled when the freeway was built in the 1970s. Nevada Brewery's cave, however, is still there and is used for tours and events.

RED LEDGE STAMP MILL

Donated to the City of Grass Valley by the Red Ledge Mine (located near the little town of Washington, California), this three-stamp mill was dedicated to the "Cousin Jack" miners, who came to Grass Valley from Cornwall, England. Today, this monument is located on the corner of Main and South Auburn Streets in downtown Grass Valley.

WOMEN OF THE GOLD RUSH ERA

Of the approximately 40,000 people who arrived by ship in the San Francisco harbor in 1849, only about 700 were women. Of these 700 women, most accompanied their husbands, but some (single or widowed) traveled to California to find economic opportunities and adventure. Others arrived in the harbor because their husbands had sent for them. During the journey to San Francisco, many people died from diseases, such as cholera and fever, while others perished in accidents. Sadly, some women became widowed while traveling to California. Those who arrived with their husbands often became widows due to mining accidents, diseases and violent disputes between miners.

The women who made it to California, especially those who were single or widowed, had to find a way to support themselves and their children, if they had any. Many became saloon owners, boardinghouse owners and teachers (if there were enough children to be schooled)—others became prostitutes. The gold rush was not an easy time, but it was often most difficult for women who were on their own.

ALPHA AND OMEGA HYDRAULIC DIGGINS

Eighteen miles east of Nevada City, just off of Highway 20, is the Alpha-Omega overlook rest stop. Located there are California Historic Landmarks Nos. 628 and 629. These landmarks refer to the Alpha and Omega Hydraulic Diggins, which can be seen to the north.

Alpha and Omega were two small mining towns that were located just one mile apart. They were settled in the 1850s, and the world-famous opera star Emma Nevada was born in Alpha. Today, the towns are long gone, but the nearby scars from the hydraulic diggings serve as reminders of their roles in the area's local mining history.

THE LOCAL ECONOMY FLOURISHED

The profits from the gold mines helped reinvigorate California's economy. The strengthening economy, combined with dramatic and sudden population increases, led California to become the thirty-first state on September 9, 1850. California was officially and literally on the map.

At the height of California's gold production, its mines ran for 364 days a year, 24 hours a day. The crushing noise from the mines was only absent for one day a year—not for Christmas, but for the annual Miner's Picnic. People were so accustomed to hearing the loud sound of ore being crushed at the stamp mills that, when it did stop, the quiet was upsetting to them, as it often meant that there had been an accident at the mines.

In the early 1860s, after hydraulic mining had been outlawed, Northern California's population started to decline. However, the large hard rock mining operations that surrounded Nevada City and Grass Valley continued to flourish. The mines provided jobs and a strong local economy. These small mining towns often contained retail stores, trading posts, hotels, transportation depots, doctors' offices, dentists' offices, saloons, bakeries and schools, which created bustling communities in the Sierra Nevada Foothills.

The wine industry was a part of this local economy, and at times, it was a fairly large part. Around the same time that hydraulic mining (which had been very profitable) was outlawed, people began to realize that gold mining in general was not going to be the money maker that many had expected it to be. Northern California residents soon began turning to agriculture as an alternative to gold mining. Vineyards became truly successful in this region, and they made enough money to support a large number of families in the area.

In the late nineteenth century, there was a rivalry of sorts between Nevada City and Grass Valley that dated back to the area's gold mining days. At that time, Nevada City was reserved for management and the city's "upper crust," which included mine owners, lawyers, doctors and other professionals. The miners and other "blue-collar" workers typically lived in Grass Valley. Although that distinction is long gone today—the towns have practically grown into each other—people are still quite proud of living in one or the other, and it is doubtful that the two towns will ever officially merge. Today, the wineries in Grass Valley and Nevada City (along with the wineries in Penn Valley and Chicago Park) are not as much an individual town's winery as they are a part of the Sierra Foothills appellation.

While many Californians saw the transition from mining to agriculture as a good thing, the quick changes that were made to the California landscape as a result of this transition did not benefit everyone. Entire indigenous societies were attacked and forced off of their lands by the "forty-niners," or those who sought gold during the peak year of the gold rush, 1849. The first people to reach the gold fields in the spring of 1848 were California residents (although California was not yet an official state). These people were primarily agriculturally oriented Americans and Europeans, and they were accompanied by some Native Americans and Spanish-speaking Californians. In late 1848, the first people to arrive from out of state were generally from Oregon, the Sandwich Islands (Hawaii) and Latin America. Of the estimated 300,000 people who arrived in California to look for their fortunes, half of them came by sea, and the other half came over land on the California Trail and the Gila River Trail.

While most of the first "forty-niners" were Americans, over time, thousands of people traveled to California from Europe, Australia, Latin America and China. These miners often brought their entire families, and women and children of all ethnicities often panned for gold right alongside the men. Some of the more enterprising families set up boardinghouses to accommodate the large influx of men into California. The boardinghouse owners often made more money than the gold miners they housed, as they provided a service that was in very high demand.

Many of the people who made the journey to California to find their fortunes faced significant hardships. Most of them traveled a great distance, oftentimes leaving their wives and children behind, to find prosperity. Once their riches came (if they ever did), these men would send for their families to join them in California. Many of the men who came by sea had to travel through the port in San Francisco. Most just traveled through, on to the gold fields, but some remained in San Francisco and started businesses that supported the gold trade. In 1846, San Francisco was a small settlement with a population of about 200 people, but by 1852, San Francisco had grown into a city with a population of over 36,000 people.

AARON SARGENT

Aaron Sargent, a man who was politically supported by temperance organizations, delivered a speech on August 31, 1885, inside the Nevada Theatre to dedicate the first California Agricultural Fair of the Seventeenth District (an event that is now known as the Nevada County Fair). Mr. Sargent did not speak of wine's health benefits; instead, he said, "I leave to others the task of ascertaining if a pure article of wine is injurious as a beverage." He did note, however, that "California will yet be the greatest wine-producing country in the world, and the best part of California for wine and raising grapes is among these very foothills."[35] It is amusing that he referred to California as a country. With the recent 1884 Sawyer Decision, which outlawed hydraulic mining for environmental reasons, Sargent wanted to suggest that a less destructive (and more positive) way to profit from the land was to plant vineyards. "A few generations hence, when this state will have some millions of population, all these hills will be covered with grape vines," Sargent predicted. "But that time is far distant. The serious question now is how shall the present population find the means of livelihood?"[36]

Aaron Sargent served three terms in the House of Representatives and one term in the United States Senate. Sargent also served as the minister to Germany (or more formally, the envoy extraordinary and minister plenipotentiary). His ambassadorship, which lasted from 1882 to 1884, gave him the opportunity to travel throughout Europe. During his travels, he saw the Rhine River vineyards and was convinced that grapes would grow well in western Nevada County. As he traveled along the Rhine, from Mainz to Cologne, aboard a steamer, he saw old castles—some had been restored and some were in ruins. He saw the sunny sides of hills that were stone terraced to use every available inch of space. "Up the hillsides, men and women have carried soil and fertilizer in baskets on their backs and planted the vines. In

Aaron Augustus Sargent.
Courtesy of the Union
Newspaper.

this Seventeenth District, there are vast acres entirely unoccupied, as well adapted to wine culture as the best in Germany."

During his speech, Sargent also encouraged local miners to remain in the area and to find new ways to earn a living, and he suggested that growing vineyards could be a good option. With the end of hydraulic mining, hundreds of jobs disappeared, but Sargent reminded his constituents to not be tempted to travel down to the valley in search of work when there were opportunities in the foothills. He also reminded them that "a man does not better his condition who leaves the mountains for the valleys or lower cities. I say to you, mountain men, turn your hand to whatever offers here at home, rather than take forlorn chances elsewhere."[37] Sargent clearly saw that the potential of this region was tied to the development of vineyards and wineries. "California wines are gaining a reputation for excellence in the East and to some degree in Europe." Sargent pointed out that the region's ability to ship wine on the Transcontinental Railroad made it possible for California wineries to compete with those in New York and

Ohio. Sargent also claimed that California wines were far superior to the "spurious imitations and poisonous decoctions" that were being produced in the eastern part of the United States at the time.[38] It seems that, along with his other achievements, Aaron Sargent also had the ability of foresight, as California has quite a successful wine industry today.

Aaron Sargent and his wife, Ellen Clark Sargent, were also instrumental in bringing about the ratification of the Nineteenth Amendment, which gave women the right to vote in America. However, the process they took to get this amendment passed was very long and arduous.

Aaron Sargent was elected as the district attorney of Nevada County in 1856. At this time, Sargent also became an important leader in the newly formed Republican Party. In 1860, he was named vice president of the Republican National Convention—the same convention that selected Abraham Lincoln as the party's presidential candidate. In 1860, Aaron Sargent was also elected to Congress, where he served three terms. As chairman of the House Railroad Committee in 1862, Sargent authored the Pacific Railroad Act, which authorized the construction of the Transcontinental Railroad, which was completed in May 1869.

While her husband was busy with his own political career, Ellen Clark Sargent was becoming politically ambitious herself. In 1869, Ellen founded the first women's suffrage group in Nevada City. After founding the group, Ellen attended many suffrage meetings and became a respected leader in the movement. Ellen Clark Sargent was a colleague and friend to many important national suffrage leaders, including Susan B. Anthony, who was a frequent visitor at the Sargents' home in Nevada City. For six years, Ellen served as the treasurer for the National American Woman Suffrage Association, which was the country's most influential women's rights organization at the time. She also served as an honorary president of the California Equal Suffrage Association.

Aaron Augustus Sargent was elected to the United States Senate in 1872, but he served only one term. In 1878, Senator Sargent introduced to Congress the twenty-eight words that would later make up the Nineteenth Amendment to the Constitution of the United States. Those words read:

> *The right of citizens of the United States to vote shall not be denied or abridged by the United States or by any state on account of sex.*

The bill that called for the amendment was introduced without success each year for the next forty years.

Aaron Sargent died in 1887 at the age of fifty-nine, and he was buried in Nevada City's Pioneer Cemetery on West Broad Street, just a few hundred yards from the Sargents' house. Ellen passed away in 1911, and more than one thousand people gathered at Union Square in San Francisco for her memorial service. Ellen was very highly regarded, and San Francisco's mayor, A.P. McCarthy, ordered for all of the city's flags to be flown at half-staff in her honor. Ellen was buried in San Francisco.

On June 4, 1919, the Nineteenth Amendment was passed by Congress, and on August 18, 1920, it was ratified by the Senate—women were officially given the right to vote. The words of the amendment were those of Aaron Sargent and his wife, Ellen, which they had written and introduced to Congress forty years earlier. It is sad to think that they both passed before they were able to see their efforts come to fruition—before women were given the right to vote.[39]

5

The Big Three Gold Mines

As the smaller mining claims began to run dry, the larger mining companies thrived. Grass Valley eventually had three large gold mines: the Empire Mine, the North Star Mine and the Idaho-Maryland Mine. Grass Valley truly was the center of hard rock mining.[40]

While most of the miners from Cornwall preferred to drink beer, they definitely had a thirst for wine. In fact, many of California's vineyards were established with grapevines that were brought to the state by miners. At first, the predominantly Italian and French miners enjoyed their wine, and the wealthier mine owners and managers served it while entertaining guests.

EMPIRE MINE STATE HISTORIC PARK

Empire Mine State Historic Park was once the site of one of the largest, richest and longest-running gold mines (1850–1956) in California. The mine produced 5.8 million ounces of gold, which, in 2019, would be valued at more than $8 billion.[41]

Stretching out over 856 acres, this state park beautifully tells the rich story of hard rock gold mining. There, hard rock miners worked underground in vertical and near vertical mine shafts that plunged beneath the surface of the

Model replica of the Empire-Star Mine Complex, which dates back to 1938. *Author photograph.*

earth. In this area, gold was primarily found in quartz, which was located deep underground. Today, 367 miles of these deep mine shafts remain and form a very impressive maze. Inside Empire Mine State Historic Park's welcome center, visitors can view a scale replica of all the underground mine shafts that run underneath Grass Valley. The replica also has reference tabs that point out current locations and businesses. After seeing this network of mineshafts, visitors often wonder how the town hasn't collapsed. One theory for this is that the area's water tables have continuously filled the mineshafts with water.

But what led to the creation of this beautiful park? A man named George Roberts first discovered the Ophir Hill vein of gold, which eventually became the Empire Mine. The Empire Mine, along with the Idaho-Maryland Mine and the North Star Mine, ended up producing nearly $300 million worth of gold at the prices of the time. Roberts founded the Empire Mine in 1850 but sold it in 1852 to the Empire Company, which managed other mines in the area. Controlling interest in the Empire Mine changed hands several times throughout the 1850s and 1860s. By 1869, a man named

William Bourn Sr. held the controlling interest in the Empire Mine. The Bourn family maintained control of the mine until 1929, when Newmont Mining purchased it for $250,000. In April 1975, Newmont sold the mine property to the state of California for $1.25 million, and the California Parks department turned it into the most visited (and most prized) mine from the California Gold Rush.[42]

In 1905, the Empire Mine adopted a more efficient mining method in which cyanide was used to dissolve gold while it was still embedded in quartz. Once it was dissolved the gold was then removed from the quartz in liquid form. Today, this method is still used by gold mines around the world. At this time, miners also had to manually move heavy ore-filled cars until mules were introduced to the gold mines. As one of the most efficiently operated gold mines in the United States, the Empire Mine listed the use of mules among its many industry improvements. While the miners appreciated the assistance, the mules did not have a very comfortable existence. The working mules lived in underground barns until they became too old to be productive.

Although the Empire Mine was able to support itself and its employees, it was not able to fully flourish until San Francisco businessman William B. Bourn Sr. acquired a controlling interest in 1869. Not long after Mr. Bourn's sudden death in 1874, production at the Empire Mine decreased, which was unfortunate. In 1879, Mr. Bourn's then-twenty-two-year-old son, William B. Bourn Jr., took over management of the mine. He was able to keep the Empire Mine from closing, and under his direction, it was once again able to turn a profit. William B. Bourn Jr. was also able to push several of the mine's shafts past the 1,200-foot level; until then, this was considered to be the maximum depth of a mine shaft.[43]

William Bourn Jr. had a younger cousin named George W. Starr. He was only nineteen years old when he began working at the mine in 1881, but by 1887, George had gone from being a "mucker" (loading rocks and ore into cars) to the superintendent of the mine. In 1893, George Starr, who was considered a mining genius by then, left the Empire Mine to go work in South Africa's gold mines. Several years later, when Starr visited San Francisco, Bourn convinced his cousin to return to the Empire Mine, where Starr worked for another thirty years.

Possibly the most important factors in the success of California's hard rock mining were the skilled miners who immigrated to the region from Cornwall, England. In Cornwall, hard rock tin and copper mining had been practiced for more than one thousand years. When they arrived in

Gold miners at the 2,200-foot level of the Empire Mine prior to 1906. *Courtesy of the California Historical Society Collection at University of Southern California.*

California, these Cornishmen brought with them skill, experience and the latest mining technology and equipment. The Cornish pump was one such invention; it was so efficient at removing water that it was used until the 1930s. In California, Cornish miners dug 367 miles of tunnels—some traveled for nearly a full vertical mile below the surface.[44]

By 1929, the Empire Mine had combined with the North Star Mine and became known as Empire-Star Mines Ltd. It was then sold to Newmont Mining, and it produced enough gold to keep the effects of the Great Depression away from western Nevada County. There truly was no depression in the region due to the gold mines—it was just a story that people read about in the local newspapers.

The mine was closed during World War II, when many of its employees were enlisted in the armed forces. The government had also closed all of the gold mines, because they were "not critical to the war effort."[45] The mine was reopened in 1945, after the war, but gold was still valued at its 1934 price—$35 per troy ounce. At the time, it unfortunately cost more per ounce to bring gold to the surface than it was worth. The mining efforts in California did not stop completely, but they were decreasing steadily until the Empire Mine was officially closed in 1956. In its lifetime, the Empire Mine yielded nearly 6 million troy ounces of gold.[46]

Today's visitors to the Empire Mine State Historic Park can look down the main shaft of California's richest gold mine, and they can even descend a few feet to see what it may have been like to be a miner at the Empire Mine. Visitors can also tour the mine's yard buildings that have been preserved, and they can visit the blacksmith shop, where experienced blacksmiths can often be found demonstrating their crafts.

Looking down the mine shaft at Empire Mine, where the miners worked. *Author photograph.*

Visitors to the mine can also see displays of stamp mills and other pieces of gold mining equipment. The grounds are beautifully manicured, with seasonal blooms, including a large rose garden that is usually in full bloom in May.

Amidst the park's lush, beautiful gardens is an impressive stone cottage, where William Bourn Jr., the wealthy mine owner, and his family spent a lot of time. San Francisco architect Willis Polk designed the English manor–style cottage and gardens. It was constructed using waste rock from the mine, blending utility and style. Built in 1897, the home was referred to as the "Cottage" in an effort to distinguish it from Mr. Bourn's other homes. Unlike many other homes that were constructed in the early

A front view of Bourn Cottage. *Author photograph.*

1900s, this cottage was equipped with electric lights, which were powered by the mine's electric system. Inside, the cottage was finished in a beautiful clear heart redwood; the main floor holds the kitchen, service rooms, living room, dining room and a reading room, which was later used as a bedroom by Bourn Jr. The second floor of the cottage contained four bedrooms and two bathrooms, and the servants' rooms and bathroom were located above the kitchen. Docent-led tours are available at the Cottage during special park events, and they are highly recommended.

Another notable building located on the grounds of the Empire Mine State Historic Park is the Empire Clubhouse. William Bourn Jr. built the clubhouse in 1905 for his supervisors to use; he also used it as a place to entertain guests. Today, it is used by the Empire Country Club and for special park events.

Throughout the year, Empire Mine State Historic Park periodically presents its Living History Days, which are hosted by park rangers and volunteer docents. Often, these rangers and volunteers wear authentic costumes from the time periods they are representing. The rangers and volunteers give wonderful tours of the Bourn Cottage and share many

The clubhouse at the Empire Mine State Historic Park. *Author photograph.*

The mine manager's office at the Empire Mine. *Author photograph.*

stories with guests. It is a spectacular way to see the park and experience what it may have been like to live in the cottage all those years ago.[47]

Another noteworthy building in the park is the mine manager's office. This restored 1898 building was used while both William Bourn Jr. and the Newmont Mining Corporation owned the mine.

NORTH STAR MINE

The North Star Mine, which encompasses over seven hundred acres of land in Grass Valley, is located on Old Auburn Road. In 1851, a rich gold vein was discovered two miles south of Grass Valley by a party of French miners; this vein came to be known as the Lafayette Hill Claim. Between 1851 and 1956, the property was very active, with two main mine shafts and several operational buildings and stamp mills on site. In 1860, two brothers, Edward and John Coleman, bought controlling interest in the mine, and in 1867, they joined a conglomeration of mines in the area that became known as the North Star Mining Company. William Bourn II, the owner of the Empire Mine, purchased the North Star Mine in 1883. In 1886, the main incline shaft traveled down 1,500 feet, and a forty-stamp mill was built on old Auburn Road. Bourn created a new water system to supply both the Empire Mine and the North Star Mine. The mine water was moved by Cornish pumps, and a Pelton water wheel supplied the power.[48]

In 1895, Arthur deWint Foote was hired as an engineer at the North Star Mine. While he was there, he developed the North Star Powerhouse, which provided electricity to the mines, and he was eventually promoted to general manager. Arthur was married to noted author and illustrator Mary Hallock Foote. Together, they commissioned the now-famous architect Julia Morgan (designer of the Hearst Castle and other famous structures) to design a large mansion on the North Star Mine's grounds.[49] Today, that home is called the North Star House, and it is being restored. It is still used for events such as weddings, fundraisers and seasonal farmers markets.

NORTH STAR MINE POWERHOUSE AND PELTON WHEEL MUSEUM

The North Star Mine Powerhouse and Pelton Wheel Museum is located at the end of Mill Street, on the corner of Allison Ranch Road and McCourtney Road. It is in an area that was once referred to as Boston Ravine in Grass Valley and recognized as California Landmark No. 843. It has also been recognized as the most complete hard rock mining museum in all of California.

Operated by the Nevada County Historical Society, the museum is located in a building that was once the powerhouse for the North Star Mine. The building was constructed in 1895 on the edge of Wolf Creek. The museum is in a beautiful setting, and it is a nice place to have a picnic before or after a tour. The North Star Mine was within a couple of miles of this powerhouse, close to the current location of the North Star House.

Mining equipment on display outside of the North Star Powerhouse and Pelton Wheel Museum in Grass Valley. *Author photograph.*

Above: A front view of
the Bourn Cottage.
Author photograph.

Left: Firehouse No. 1
Museum in Nevada
City. *Author photograph.*

A winter sunset on Scott's Flat Lake. *Author photograph.*

Clusters of red wine grapes show the fruit's depth of color. *Author photograph.*

Truckee River near historic downtown Truckee. *Author photograph.*

Left: 1853 Wells Fargo and Co. building in French Corral. *Courtesy of Elias Funez.*

Below: Covered Bridge at Bridgeport. *Watercolor painting by Nevada City artist Loana Beason.*

Looking up Broad Street in downtown Nevada City. *Watercolor painting by artist Loana Beeson.*

A replica of a Nevada County Traction Company trolley car. *Author photograph.*

Above: A painted mural of the narrow-gauge railroad that is located inside the Northern Mines Building at the Nevada County Fairgrounds. *Artist, Albert Krebs. Author photograph with permission of the Nevada County Fairgrounds.*

Left: Rob Chrisman getting ready to plant a grapevine in a hole he just dug. *Courtesy of Marilyn Chrisman.*

The "View Forever" at Lucchesi Vineyard. *Courtesy of Mario Clough.*

Mario Clough, the co-owner (with his wife, Linda) of Lucchesi Winery and Vineyards, sits and appreciates his wine and the winery's beautiful setting. *Author photograph.*

Phil Starr giving a vineyard tour at Sierra Starr Vineyards and Winery. *Author photograph.*

Buttermaker's Cottage in Western Gateway Park in Penn Valley. *Courtesy of Nancy Peirce.*

Grape cluster ready for harvest. *Author photograph.*

Location of the Bierwagen's Happy Apple Kitchen restaurant and Farm Market. *Author photograph.*

Left: Phil Starr pouring wine into his concrete egg at Sierra Starr Winery. *Courtesy of Jackson Starr.*

Below: The beautiful grounds at Naggiar Vineyards and Winery. *Author photograph.*

Naggiar Vineyards. *Courtesy of Mary Naggiar.*

Mike Naggiar explaining how grapes are grown to a tour group. *Author photograph.*

Montoliva Vineyard's view of the red barn. *Author photograph.*

Award-winning wines on display at Montoliva's tasting room. *Author photograph.*

Nevada City wines in the cup of a Pelton Wheel. *Courtesy of Kim Crevoiserat.*

Nevada City Winery's large tasting room. *Courtesy of Kim Crevoiserat.*

Russ Jones, the owner of the Truckee River Winery, pressing grapes in the late 1990s. *Courtesy of Truckee River Winery.*

Gray Pine Vineyard in Penn Valley. *Author photograph.*

Guy Lauterbach, a vineyard owner and winemaker, greeting guests in his Gray Pine tasting room. *Author photograph.*

A replica of an Old West town in Rough and Ready, which belongs to Dr. and Mrs. Jacobitz. The horse's name is Brady. *Author photograph.*

Montoliva Vineyards. *Author photograph.*

Clavey Vineyards. *Courtesy of Clavey Vineyards.*

A side view of the North Star Gold Quartz Mill circa 1910. *Courtesy of the California Historical Society Collection at University of Southern California.*

The Pelton wheel stands thirty feet tall inside the North Star Mine Powerhouse and Pelton Wheel Museum in Grass Valley. *Author photograph.*

At the North Star Mine Powerhouse and Pelton Wheel Museum, visitors can view a thirty-foot Pelton wheel that is on display—it is the world's largest. Pelton wheels were invented by Lester Pelton, and the particular wheel that is on display in the museum was built by A.D. Foote in 1895. In the late nineteenth century, the Pelton wheel was used to turn water into electricity. As the cups on the wheels scooped water, the wheels turned and generated energy. Another interesting exhibit in the museum is a mining skip (similar to a rail car that could descend almost vertically) that was used to carry men down into the mines. The museum also has a Cornish pump that was used to remove water from mine shafts.[50]

IDAHO-MARYLAND MINE

The Idaho-Maryland Mine, located in the Grass Valley mining district of Northern California, was one of the most productive and well-known gold mines in the United States. The mine was opened in 1863 and was located near the corner of Brunswick Road and East Bennett Street. It was reportedly the second-largest gold mine in the United States in 1941 (second only to the North Star and Empire Mine Complex). The Idaho-Maryland produced up to 129,000 ounces of gold per year until 1942, when it was forced to shut down by the U.S. government.[51] At that time, all of the gold mines in the United States were shut down by the government, as the armed forces' need for copper shifted the national mining workforce from gold to copper production.

The Idaho Maryland Mine in Grass Valley around 1895. Note the narrow-gauge railroad tracks in the foreground. *Courtesy of the California Historical Society Collection at University of Southern California.*

Idaho Maryland hard rock miners at the 2,000-foot elevation on an electric trolley pulling ore cars. *Courtesy of the California Historical Society Collection at University of Southern California.*

In its lifetime, the Idaho-Maryland Mine produced a total of 2.4 million ounces of gold. Today, the mine represents a consolidation of a number of important early mines, including the Idaho, Maryland, Brunswick, Eureka and Union Hill Mines.

SMALLER GOLD MINES

There were many other small mines and mining towns in the area, and most of them had very interesting names, including Blue Tent, You Bet, Rough and Ready, Red Dog, French Corral and Scott's Flat. These were all just the beginnings of dozens of mining camps that grew from wild and rough tent communities to bustling new towns with businesses, schools and churches. Now, the only things that remain from most of these mining communities are road names, although Rough and Ready has survived as a small town of

Scott's Flat Lake, just outside of Nevada City. *Author photograph.*

its own in the area west of Penn Valley and east of Grass Valley. Scott's Flat was once a Scottish mining community comprised of just a few thousand people, but it is now under water—under a reservoir called Scott's Flat Lake. This lake is located just east of Nevada City.

By the end of the gold rush, California had gone from a lightly populated ex-Mexican territory to a state. And in 1856, it even had one of its first two U.S. senators, John C. Frémont, selected to be the first presidential nominee for the newly formed Republican Party. California had come a long way in a relatively short period of time. And in that time, it had been proven that the Sierra Nevada Foothills were perfect for growing wine grapes.

There's So Much More than Gold

While so much of Nevada County's history revolves around the gold rush, there is so much more to the area's story. It has a rich transportation history, and it has experienced a number of agricultural milestones and a couple of "firsts" that are quite significant. Transportation and agriculture have had a huge impact on the area's local vineyards.

THE NARROW GAUGE RAILROAD

In the early days of the gold rush, mule trains outfitted with supplies for the mines would set out from Sacramento and travel to the gold mines in western Nevada County. Once they reached the gold mines and delivered the supplies, those same mule trains would haul gold back to Sacramento so that it could be deposited in Wells Fargo and other San Francisco banks. This form of transportation was slow; the wagons could only hold so much, and in winter, the narrow dirt roads were often impassable.[52]

The Central Pacific Railroad reached Colfax in 1865. At that time, the railroads began to transport the food and supplies that were needed in the mines and their surrounding communities from San Francisco, to Sacramento and then to Colfax. This was a much faster and more efficient mode of transportation than the mule trains, but it was soon obvious that a railroad line from Colfax to Grass Valley and Nevada City was necessary.

At this time, Nevada County also had a thriving lumber industry that needed a new transportation option, as lumber was in high demand for use in construction. California's fruit, especially Bartlett pears and tokay grapes that were grown in local orchards and vineyards in and around Chicago Park, also needed to be transported to Colfax. There, the fruit would be transferred to refrigerated cars on the Central Pacific Railroad, where it would then make its way to market on both the Pacific and Atlantic coasts. The ability to transport wine grapes this way allowed vineyard owners to sell their excess grapes to other wineries, including those in Sonoma Valley and Napa Valley.

Passengers in Northern California also needed an efficient mode of transportation. Salesmen who traveled between mining camps and towns wanted quick and easy ways to get there. The residents of Nevada County who needed to travel to Sacramento and San Francisco—either to attend a business meeting, the opera or a theater performance or to consult a medical professional and shop—also wanted faster transportation. At that time, there was also a need to transport the high school children of Colfax to Nevada City, as Colfax did not have a high school at that time. Colfax's students traveled to Nevada City at the beginning of the week and returned at the end of the week. While they were in Nevada City, the students stayed with either friends or family members, and some stayed in special student residences during the school week.

Since there was an apparent need for local transportation, the Nevada County Narrow Gauge Railroad Company was incorporated on April 4, 1874, and it was headquartered in Grass Valley. After two years of construction, in

A Chicago Park fruit packing shed, where fruit was prepared for shipment to Colfax on the narrow-gauge railroad, circa the early 1900s. *Courtesy of the California Historical Society Collection at University of Southern California.*

Narrow-gauge train tracks. *Author photograph.*

1876, the company's passenger and commercial rail line opened and provided transportation for goods and passengers between the Nevada City and Grass Valley areas to the Central Pacific Line in Colfax, California. All at once, everything was easier to move over land—supplies were easily transported, gold was taken to banks and people were taken to where they wanted to go.

Many may wonder why this railroad was referred to as a narrow-gauge line. This was due to the fact that the width of the tracks (the gauge) was just 3 feet, which is narrower than the standard rails of the time, which were 4 feet and 8.5 inches wide. Narrow-gauge railways were often used because they were less expensive to build and operate, especially in mountainous and difficult terrain. Narrow-gauge railways were usually built with tighter curves, smaller structure gauges and lighter rails. They were often constructed to serve communities in which the traffic potential did not justify the cost of a standard-gauge line.[53] It is estimated that the construction and equipment needed to run the Nevada County Narrow Gauge Railroad would have cost $411,132. Only one bid was submitted for the construction of the Nevada County Narrow Gauge Railroad; it was for $500,000 and was submitted by M.F. Beatty. Beatty received a lump sum payment of $500,000, and

Nevada County's narrow-gauge railroad on the Bear River Bridge, near Colfax, in 1895. *Courtesy of the California Historical Society Collection at University of Southern California.*

construction of the rail line started in January 1875. Turton and Knox were subcontracted for earthwork. John Flint Kidder was the chief engineer. Within two months, six hundred men were hired to construct the railroad.[54]

The construction of the Nevada County Narrow Gauge Railroad included two bridges, five trestles and two tunnels. After leaving the Colfax station, the railroad headed north, crossed Bear River and crossed the Nevada County line. One of the line's first stations was in the town of You Bet, which serviced the Goodwin Drift Gravel Mine. After passing You Bet, the railroad proceeded to Chicago Park, a fruit and wine grape growers' colony. The rail line then continued into Grass Valley. A second contractor, J.K. Bynre, was brought in to replace the first contractor, Beatty, who was unable to complete the project. The construction of the railroad was completed in the spring of 1876, and the inaugural train ride from Colfax to Grass Valley took place on April 11. The line's first train reached Nevada City on May 20.[55]

THE KIDDER FAMILY

John Flint Kidder was born in 1830 in New York City. He was a politician, civil engineer and railroad executive, and he married Sarah Clark in 1874. The couple moved to Grass Valley in 1875, when John was offered the position of chief engineer over the construction of the Nevada County Narrow Gauge Railroad. Construction of the rail line was completed in 1876, and John Kidder became the railroad's general superintendent in 1877. He worked for the railroad's first president, John C. Coleman, who had been the president of the North Star Mine. By 1884, John Kidder was the president of the railroad (he was also the secretary and treasurer), and he made his family members the board of directors.[56]

John and Sarah Kidder lived in a lovely mansion near the Grass Valley rail station. Sarah was known for her lovely parties and her house—it was one of the first "modern" homes in the area at that time, and it had the first concrete sidewalk in Grass Valley. Sarah also volunteered at an orphan society, where she eventually adopted a daughter named Beatrice.[57] John Kidder, who suffered from diabetes, died in Grass Valley in April 1901 at the age of seventy-one. His wife, Sarah Kidder, stepped into his role at the Nevada County Narrow Gauge Railroad and became the world's first female president of a railroad.

Sarah Clark Kidder was born in 1839, and she spent twelve years serving as the president of the Nevada County Narrow Gauge Railroad. By all accounts, she ran a very profitable railroad during that time. Under her watch, the Nevada County Narrow Gauge Railroad (NCNGRR) converted its locomotives from those that used steam to those that used oil as fuel, which reduced the need for frequent stops to take on extra wood and water and shortened the time of the railroad's trips. By 1912, the NCNGRR was running three mixed trains every day—each way, between Nevada City and Colfax—and a fourth mixed train that ran between Grass Valley and Colfax. Initially, the railroad's rate for passenger transport was just ten cents per mile, and freight services cost twenty cents per ton, per mile.[58] Notable passengers on the Nevada County Narrow Gauge included U.S. presidents Ulysses S. Grant and Theodore Roosevelt, Britain's Prince Albert and singer Emma Nevada.[59] In 1913, Sarah Kidder sold all of her stock in the railroad and moved to San Francisco, where she passed away in 1933 at the age of ninety-four.[60]

While the railroad operated on steam, its twenty-two-mile route took two hours to complete, as several stops were necessary along the way to load wood for the engine and to bring on more water for the boiler that produced the steam. The route climbed in elevation, from Colfax at 2,421 feet to

Kidder family portrait. Sarah (*left*), Beatrice (*center*) and John (*right*). *Courtesy of the N.C.N.G.R.R. Transportation Museum.*

A replica of the Nevada County Narrow Gauge Railroad's caboose #1, which was built between 1984 and 1986 by John Christensen at his home in Nevada City. The original caboose was scrapped when the railroad was closed in 1942. *Author photograph.*

Nevada City at 2,800 feet. The line also crossed the Bear River on the then-highest railroad bridge in California. The line crossed the Greenhorn Creek as it flowed toward the west in deep, narrow canyons.

The NCNGRR made stops in the tiny settlements of Chicago Park and Buena Vista. At the time, Chicago Park only had a railroad station, a grocery store and a post office. It was the center for the area's widespread agricultural community. The Buena Vista station was located in a broad meadow near Grass Valley. Only a few homes were grouped near the station. Today, the area that was once known as Buena Vista, is referred to as Peardale. It is a lovely residential and agricultural community between Chicago Park and Grass Valley. The Grass Valley station was located on the east side of town; it had a long station house, a freight and passenger depot, a machine shop, a blacksmith shop, oil tanks, warehouses and the Kidder Mansion. The station also had a fifty-foot turntable that required two men to turn a locomotive by hand.[61] Today, those buildings are gone, but remnants of the train tracks can still be seen near the corner of East Bennett and Kidder Streets.

A train parked in front of the Kidder Mansion in Grass Valley on the Nevada County Narrow Gauge Railroad. *Courtesy of the Searls Historical Library, PIC5 Tra-Nar Eng#1 19b.*

A painted mural of the narrow-gauge railroad by artist Albert Krebs. It is now kept inside of the Northern Mines Building at the Nevada County Fairgrounds. *Artist, Albert Krebs. Author photograph with permission of the Nevada County Fairgrounds.*

Nevada County Traction Company's trolley no. 4 makes a turn from Mill Street onto East Main Street in Grass Valley. *Courtesy of the California Historical Society Collection at University of Southern California.*

For sixty-six years, the Nevada County Narrow Gauge Railroad hauled more than $200 million worth of gold, along with mining machinery, lumber, petroleum and merchandise. It also provided passenger transportation but often with a separate train that ran on a different schedule from the shipping train. Sometimes, the railroad trains did not run according to schedule, which earned the line the nickname "Never Come, Never Go."[62]

The Nevada County Narrow Gauge Railroad was the only railroad in the West that was never robbed, even though its primary function was to transport gold to San Francisco for processing. The railroad's builder and owner, John Flint Kidder, had a reputation that he would personally hunt down and kill anyone who ever tried to rob his rail line.[63]

In 1938, the Nevada County Narrow Gauge Railroad's passenger services were suspended due to dwindling traffic, and in 1940, the Grass Valley Depot and the Kidder Mansion suffered extensive damage in a fire. After the start of World War II, the rail line was sold for scrap metal; for $251,000, the line's locomotives were either scrapped or sold to other narrow-gauge railroads. The last train that ever traveled over these tracks ran on May 29, 1942.[64]

THE SOUTH YUBA RIVER STATE PARK

While gold was first discovered on a creek near Grass Valley, it was soon discovered in the South Yuba River as well. There were many mining claims along the South Yuba River, and many of the miners who worked them were the first to bring grapevines to the area. The river was a major water source for agriculture, which included the grapes that were planted within the river's range.

Stretching for twenty miles between Bridgeport (to the north of Penn Valley) and Malakoff Diggins State Park (northeast of Nevada City), the South Yuba River State Park is breathtakingly beautiful, wild and scenic.

Bridgeport is the site of the United States' largest single-span covered bridge. Both a State and National Historic Landmark, the Bridgeport Bridge was built in 1862. It was a well-traveled route that was used to bring cattle, gold and travelers through the area. Approximately one hundred freight wagons used the turnpike and the bridge in the 1860s. The turnpike continued to operate until 1901.[65]

The Bridgeport Covered Bridge in 2007, before current preservation efforts. *Author photograph.*

A view from inside the covered bridge, looking toward the red barn. *Author photograph.*

Ranching was started in Bridgeport in 1862, when Charles Cole arrived in the area. He built Bridgeport House, which served as a residence and hostelry at the time. It is also thought Charles Cole built the large red barn that is so well aligned with the bridge that teams could drive directly from the bridge to the barn and vice versa.[66] In 1971, as part of a previous restoration project, the length of the bridge was reduced from 251 to 229 feet.

TABLE 1. TOLL RATES IN 1862

8 horses, mules or ox team	$6.00
4 horses, mules or ox team	$4.00
1 horse, mule or ox	$1.75
2-horse buggy, each way	$1.50
1-horse buggy, each way	$1.00
Horseman	$0.50
Footman	$0.25
Hog or sheep	$0.05

Liquid Gold: The History of Wine in Nevada County

L ocal Nevada County wine history dates back to 1848, when Nevada County was still a part of Yuba County (Nevada County was established in 1851). The gold rush brought an influx of gold seekers from many different places (including Italy, Germany and France). These immigrants arrived with pickaxes and gold pans, and sometimes, they also arrived with their own grapevines hanging from their saddlebags.[67] As soon as towns began to spring up, grapevines were planted to help supply the thirsty miners with wine. As early as 1862, there was a saloon on Broad Street in Nevada City, serving wine to customers—wine that was grown and produced in Nevada City.

At the time, the expected yield from a field of five-year-old vines was four tons per acre. The land in Northern California was cheap, and the vineyards were cultivated with horsepower. The vineyards needed little maintenance, since the area's bone-dry summers kept the weeds under control. In his report from 1866, the county assessor estimated that one-twelfth (1,200 square miles) of Nevada County's land (60,000 square miles in the total) was suitable for growing grapes that were used for wine, brandy and raisins.[68] The soil there was primarily a combination of volcanic ash, sedimentary lava and decomposed granite and oxide of iron—making it excellent for grape cultivation.

The vineyards at that time were small—only one thousand to three thousand vines were grown on average in each vineyard. The community of French Corral was settled by the French (in particular, four men named

Ponce, Poulinier, Monier and Freschot), whose vines were planted there with good success. Mission and black Hamburg grapes produced wines similar to a claret. In the Sweetland area, mission grapes produced white wines. In Bridgeport, Louis Buhring grew mission, Hamburg, Catawba and white Muscat of Alexandria grapes. The county assessor noted, "This area develops a great deal of saccharin, which, by fermentation, is transformed into alcohol. The wines are of considerable strength—too much, perhaps, for table wines."[69]

A gentleman by the name of Francis Seibert, who owned Louis Seibert's Vineyard and Soda Works in Nevada City, won one of California's first wine awards in 1869 for his Zinfandel, which was grown on Piety Hill in Nevada City.[70] Seibert had two thousand vines that grew forty varietals; his vineyard was located a half mile south of Nevada City, according to the county assessor's report from 1866.[71]

VINEYARD OWNERS

While not all of California's vineyard owners from the mid-1800s are listed here, the following list will give you a glimpse into the kind of people who saw the benefit and potential of producing wine in Northern California. Some of the area's vineyard owners were recorded in the county assessor's report from the second half of the 1800s. They were:[72]

Charles Barker: Barker lived on the corner of Henderson Street and Colfax Avenue in 1862. There, he had twelve acres of orchards and a vineyard.

W. Bree: Bree came to America from England in 1869, when he was just twenty-nine years old. Along with his brother, he owned 1,800 acres, and 10 of these acres were occupied by orchards and vineyards.

S.B. Davenport: Davenport was an insurance agent who lived on Piety Hill in Nevada City. On his 3.5 acres of land, he grew 300 fruit trees and 1,500 grapevines, which yielded twelve tons of apples and five tons of grapes in 1878.

H.L. Hatch: Hatch lived on Vine Hill in Indian Springs, Penn Valley. There, he owned 240 acres of land, 25 of which were occupied by a vineyard. Hatch also produced his own wine and served one term in the state legislature after being elected in 1865.

By 1870, there were over 450,000 vines growing in western Nevada County on several hundred acres' worth of vineyards. At this point in time, wine was sold for roughly $2 per gallon, which was a respectable price. The wines that were grown and produced in California were of very good quality. E.G. Waite produced a wine that some said was comparable to French clarets. Wine grapes were becoming a very large and important part of Nevada County's agricultural industry. In fact, E.G. Waite believed that "gold was an important source of livelihood in Nevada County, but that it wouldn't last, and that wines would be the more important and the 'perpetual source' of importance here."[73]

As the table from the county assessor indicates, the peak of the wine industry from the second half of the 1800s declined significantly in 1875.[74]

TABLE 2. TABLE OF GRAPE VINES AND GALLONS OF WINE PRODUCED

Year	# Grape Vines in County	# Gallons of Wine Produced
1860	9,000	no record
1866	124,000	10,000
1870	450,000	50,000
1875	34,000	12,000
1879	30,000	12,000

In the 1880s, after the end of the Civil War and the economic downturn that followed, there was another decade of vineyard growth in Nevada County. Yes, the demand for California's wine did increase, but at the same time, it also became popular for gentleman farmers to plant vineyards and produce wine. The quality of the grapes grown in California and the wine produced there remained very good. Nevada County grapes were well known and prized for their intense flavor and robust color. They were so popular that even some Napa winemakers bought Nevada County grapes to use in their wine production.

Cornish miners, who came to Northern California to work in the gold mines, preferred beer to wine. However, there were a good number of German and Italian settlers who came to the area in the late 1800s and brought a love of wine with them. Several families, including the Bierwagens, Locatellis and Personenis, were heavily involved in Nevada

A grape cluster ready for harvest. *Author photograph.*

County's vineyards and wineries in the early 1900s, and these families are still important to the community today.

By 1887, there were at least seventeen recognized grape growers in Nevada County. Ten of those growers also produced their own wines. One of these wineries was Nevada City Winery, which was not exactly the same as today's Nevada City Winery, but it definitely led the way in the development of Nevada County's wine industry and produced eight thousand gallons of wine in 1889.

PROHIBITION

So, what happened in the years (almost one hundred of them) that separated the wineries of the late 1800s and the late 1900s? While some may assume that Prohibition put a complete stop to Nevada County's wine industry, that isn't necessarily the case.[75] First of all, one has to look at what Prohibition was all about. It made the act of commercially produced alcohol (including wine) illegal. As should have been expected, making the production of alcohol illegal did not cause it to cease. Interest in home winemaking soared; it usually flew under the radar of those who enforced Prohibition, mostly because it was not illegal to make wine for personal consumption—or for the church.

There were definitely moral conflicts between the moral crusaders, the alcohol industry and consumers in the early 1900s. In 1906, the Anti-Saloon League (ASL) started a campaign to ban the sale of alcohol at the state level. Their speeches, public demonstrations and advertisements claimed that banning the sale of alcohol would rid society of poverty, immoral behavior and violence. They also claimed that banning the sale of alcohol would inspire new forms of sociability between men and women and that families would be happier—overall, they claimed that the world would be a better place.[76] However, the ban on alcohol sales did not keep people from consuming it. Instead, it drove the alcohol industry underground, where it was less likely to be discovered. People made alcohol at home. Saloons were converted into speakeasies in order to survive and prosper.

Alcohol has been a part of American history since the beginning. It wasn't always refined, and sometimes, it was downright dangerous to drink. At the same time, the temperance movement had always been simmering, and the battle between the two came to a head by 1919. Those who belonged to the temperance movement believed that a ban on the sale of alcohol would greatly reduce poverty and other societal issues. The amendment was proposed to Congress on December 18, 1917, and it was ratified by the required number of states on January 16, 1919. However, it did not take effect until January 16, 1920.[77] The Eighteenth Amendment to the U.S. Constitution declared that the production, transport and sale of intoxicating liquors was illegal. Though, it did not outlaw the actual consumption of alcohol. Saloons that had served alcoholic beverages were converted overnight into social clubs, soda shops and pool halls—or so it seemed.

The production of alcohol went underground. A loophole in the Eighteenth Amendment allowed each home to produce two hundred gallons of non-intoxicating cider and fruit juice per year, so thousands of otherwise law-abiding citizens became home winemakers and bootleggers. The law read "non-intoxicating," not "non-alcoholic," and the federal police were way too preoccupied with bootleggers to track what happened in private homes.[78] Prices for fresh grapes shot up, and soon, there was a shortage of available refrigerated railroad freight cars to ship them—both were caused by the increased demand. Men who needed extra income to support their families often resorted to "bootlegging," which is defined as making alcohol at home, usually with "stills." During the 1920s, and up until 1933, stills could be found in houses all over Nevada County.

By the time the nation was halfway through Prohibition, there were more grapes growing in Nevada County than there had been before Prohibition began. However, disease and phylloxera (microscopic, pale yellow, sap-sucking insects) damaged the grapevines and led to a decrease in healthy vines. Fortunately, Nevada County was, for the most part, spared from phylloxera.

The homemade liquor that was made around the United States was of very poor quality. It was made by fermenting corn, barley, wheat, yeast, sugar and other grains into alcohol. As corn became scarce, sugar was often used as a substitute in the fermentation process. Between the fear of being caught and the high demand for alcohol, bootleggers did not take time to "age" the alcohol. This alcohol was often referred to as "jackass brandy" or "bathtub gin." Homemade beer was also fermented in hidden basements and other well-hidden places. The wine, however, was of much higher quality at the time. There were Italian families in California who still had access to grapes grown in the foothills, and they continued to make homemade wine from those grapes. They were also growers, and they began replanting fine wine variety grapes, along with grape juice varieties that shipped well. Although some wineries survived by obtaining special permits to make medicinal, sacramental and non-beverage additive wines, California's overall wine production dropped by 94 percent between 1919 and 1925.

Police investigating illegal distillery equipment in 1920. The exact location of this distillery is unknown. *Courtesy of the California Historical Society Collection at University of Southern California.*

Speakeasies were careful to only permit patrons who knew the secret knock or password. To get into a speakeasy, patrons first had to know where the hidden door was located. They also had to know the password, have plenty of money and a strong stomach. Speakeasies had trap doors in their floors, hidden rooms in their basements, secret peepholes and guards. Speakeasies were not always foolproof, however, and if the "feds" raided a "joint," they usually arrested all of the owners and patrons they could catch. They also often broke open barrels that contained alcohol on site, letting the wine, whiskey or other beverage run into the streets. Sometimes, they would even take the alcohol and pour it down the sewer systems.[79]

Before Prohibition, women had not been allowed in saloons. But once the clubs went "underground," women were allowed to enter these clubs. This time was referred to as the "Roaring 20s." It was a time for new fashions—including flapper attire. Clubs began playing modern music, which led to the creation of dances like the Charleston. Public sentiment began to turn against Prohibition during the 1920s, and in 1932, the Democratic presidential nominee, Franklin D. Roosevelt, called for the repeal of the Eighteenth Amendment in his campaign.

Congress repealed Prohibition on December 5, 1933, but the taxes on alcohol remained extremely high, so bootlegging, under the table sales and organized crime continued. Prohibition came and went with little fanfare, but it devastated the wine industry. California's grape-growing, which was thriving in the 1920s, led to an over-abundance of grapes. This surplus caused the market for grapes to crash in the second half of the decade.[80] Federal agents continued to raid establishments that served alcohol, but this time, the raids were carried out to collect taxes for the U.S. government—not to stop alcohol sales or consumption.

When Prohibition ended in 1933, six wineries opened in Nevada County. Unfortunately, by that time, the demand for high-quality wine had declined. The production of large quantities of wine took priority over small, handcrafted batches. The large producers, including the Italian Swiss Colony and Gallo, were dominating the marketplace. In addition, the grapes grown in California's Central Valley were very inexpensive, and it became more difficult for Nevada County vineyards to compete.

World War II brought with it the stoppage of California's gold mining (the president declared that gold mining was not critical to the war effort) and hard times for local wineries. The one winery that was still open in the first half of the 1900s closed in the early 1950s.

8

Agriculture

More grapes are grown than any other fruit in the world. Grapevines prefer temperate climates, with warm, dry summers and mild winters. Winters of sustained cold can kill grapevines, and high humidity encourages vine disease. Perhaps this is why western Nevada County is such a good location for growing grapes. Despite this, there was much more to the area's local agriculture explosion than grapes, and there was one man in particular who is credited with being the father of agriculture in Nevada County: Felix Gillet.

FELIX GILLET

Some of Nevada County's early settlers came during the gold rush and discovered something that was perhaps more valuable than gold: agriculture.

In 1859, a twenty-four-year-old French sailor named Felix Gillet moved to Nevada City. When he arrived, Felix opened up a barber shop, which was located on Commercial Street, just below Pine Street, in downtown Nevada City. In between haircuts and shaves, Gillet sold fancy stationery, pens, toys and novelty items that he imported from France, but that was not his dream. He had another dream that changed Northern California's entire agricultural landscape.[81]

In 1869 or 1870 (sources disagree), Felix Gillet purchased sixteen acres of barren land on what was then called Aristocracy Hill; the land was located

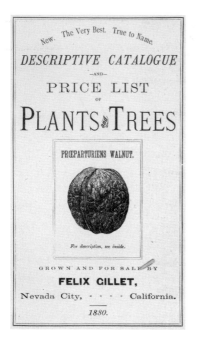

New. The Very Best. True to Name.

DESCRIPTIVE CATALOGUE
—AND—
PRICE LIST
OF
PLANTS & TREES

PRŒPARTURIENS WALNUT.

For description, see inside.

GROWN AND FOR SALE BY
FELIX GILLET,
Nevada City, - - - - California.
1880.

The cover from the 1880 edition of
Felix Gillet's *Barren Hill Nursery Catalog.*
Courtesy of the Felix Gillet Institute.

just on the outskirts of Nevada City on a road that is now known as Nursery Street. He paid $250 in gold coin for the property and placed an order for about $3,000 worth of deciduous fruit and nut trees from a nursery in France. Gillet named his property the Barren Hill Nursery and cleared and cultivated it, hauling in many loads of topsoil by hand. He also dug a well to provide water for his plants.[82]

Felix Gillet is now considered to be the father of California and the Pacific Northwest's perennial agriculture, and he is credited with importing, breeding and introducing most of the plants that now make up the foundation of California and the Pacific Northwest's perennial fruits, grapes and nuts.[83] Gillet introduced hundreds of varieties of plants that helped create these industries: almond; walnut; filbert; chestnut; cherry; apple; pear; fig; table, raisin and wine grape; plum; prune; apricot; peach; rose; nectarine; and strawberry. Many of the plants that Gillet introduced are still industry leaders, while others provided the basic genetics for further breeding that led to today's most popular crops.[84]

All of Gillet's hard work paid off, and his orchard, garden and nursery in Nevada City became a showplace. In 1884, his catalog offered 17 varieties of walnuts, 7 varieties of chestnuts, 6 varieties of filberts, 7 varieties of prunes, 55 varieties of English gooseberries and 107 varieties of grapes. The number of grape varieties offered in his catalog later grew to 241 types of grapes, including several varieties that were new to California at that time.[85] Gillet kept weather records and researched and experimented with the crops mentioned above. He also made wine, which was reportedly good, from his grapes. Gillet added to his successful venture by importing seeds and plant stock from France and other countries, which he then redistributed throughout the United States.

Some credit Felix Gillet with being the father of the English walnut industry in Northern California and Oregon. In his day, Gillet was as well-

FELIX GILLET, Proprietor Barren Hill Nursery, Nevada City, California
Grafting in Greenhouse, 1-Year Old Walnut Trees, by the Treyve Process

Showing grafted trees covered with tumblers six inches high.

Felix Gillet working in one of his greenhouses. *Courtesy of the Felix Gillet Institute.*

known as Luther Burbank and was ranked as a close second to Burbank in important developments in California's agriculture. Felix Gillet died in 1908, and he was buried in the Pioneer Cemetery in Nevada City. A bronze plaque was placed on the wall of Nevada City's city hall to honor Felix Gillet as one of the pioneer councilmen in the first city hall. Another plaque was placed at Nursery Street, and it honors him for enriching the horticulture of the world through his work with walnuts, filberts, chestnuts and prunes.

Today, The Felix Gillet Institute is a 501(c)(3) nonprofit educational organization; it was founded in 2003 by Amigo Bob Cantisano to identify, preserve and propagate the best varieties of grapes still thriving in the mining camps, farms, homesteads and towns of the Sierra and beyond. These 125-year survivors have shown a great resistance to drought, harsh weather, insects and disease. They are still producing remarkable and extremely flavorful crops with little or no human assistance.[86] The Felix Gillet Institute is also creating a database of hundreds of these plants in order to identify their characteristics, locations, crop production and more. They are also propagating these plants for use by future generations of farmers, gardeners and nursery researchers.

THE BIERWAGEN FAMILY

The Bierwagen family has greatly contributed to Nevada County's agricultural industry, and they continue to do so today. Ludwig Bierwagen arrived in Chicago Park from Russia, but it wasn't gold that brought him, it was the fertile land. He missed the orchards of Russia—his childhood home—and he wanted to plant orchards in Northern California.

The Bierwagen family's journey began in a region then known as Bessarabia, which later became Moldava; it is an area of Eastern Europe, north of the Black Sea, between Romania and Ukraine. The built-up resentment between the ethnic German minorities in Russia was to encourage the family to immigrate to the United States in 1881. They first settled in South Dakota on a farm comprising hundreds of acres, but it did not compare to the fruit orchards of his childhood, so he kept looking for a better place to settle.[87]

Around the time that Ludwig became disillusioned with South Dakota, he saw an advertisement for an area called Chicago Park in California in a German-language newspaper. Because of this advertisement, in 1902, Ludwig moved his family (including son, Christian, and daughter, Wilhelmine) to a property in Chicago Park—across the road from where the Happy Apple Kitchen is located today—at 18532 Colfax Highway (Highway 174). This restaurant and farm stand are still owned by the Bierwagen family.

According to family member Robert Tangren:

> *Ludwig Bierwagen and his family, tired of the harsh weather of South Dakota and missing the orchards and vineyards of Bessarabia, made a trip to California at the turn of the century to investigate an advertisement by a Chicago company of land for sale in what is now known as Chicago Park, California.*

Ludwig's son, Christian Bierwagen, returned to South Dakota to settle a homestead, but he liked what he saw when he visited his father in Chicago

Some of the Bierwagen's orchard land along Highway 174 in Chicago Park. *Author photograph.*

The location of the Bierwagen's Happy Apple Kitchen restaurant and Farm Market. *Author photograph.*

Park. Christian purchased land nearby, on Lower Colfax Road, in 1910. The second generation of Bierwagens in California, Christian's generation, was primarily made up of farmers and stockmen. William arrived in California in the early 1900s, his brother Frederick arrived in 1921, and his brother Michael arrived in 1922 (or 1923). They were followed by their sister, Elizabeth.[88]

The third generation of Bierwagens became a part of a fruit-growing cooperative called the Colfax Fruit Growers Association, which shipped pears all across the United States. The company used Nevada County Narrow Gauge Railroad's refrigerated cars to get the fruit to Colfax and the Central Pacific Railroad.

The last surviving male of the third generation of Bierwagens in Chicago Park was Ernie Bierwagen. Ernie was born in 1915 on his family's farm that they settled in 1902. In addition to being an orchardist, Ernie's father, Christian, helped form the Nevada Irrigation District in 1921, which is still the local water district today. The water that the district brought to the family's orchards in Chicago Park increased their pear production from one thousand to six thousand boxes of fruit per year. This was a significant growth that enabled other farms and orchards in the area to thrive, since they knew that a reliable water source existed.[89] Ernie Bierwagen passed away in 2004 at the age of eighty-eight. The fourth generation of the Bierwagen family (including Chris Bierwagen, who is also currently on the Nevada Irrigation District board of directors) continues to operate the Bierwagen Donner Trail Fruit Farm, where they grow apples and other fruit and have a seasonal pumpkin patch. They also operate the Happy Apple Kitchen restaurant and a farm store—both are very popular with locals and tourists alike.

DRY FARMING

A week without water can easily kill the average human being, but a garden that goes without water for months can produce sweeter and more flavorful fruits than what can be found in most mainstream supermarkets—even in the scorching heat of the summer. Throughout California, this unconventional technique has become more popular with smaller producers of tomatoes, apples, potatoes, melons and grapes.[90]

Grapevines are one of our planet's most drought-tolerant plants. If you plant them in rich soil and provide them with a lot of water, they won't do as well as vines that are planted in poor soils with a limited amount of water. It seems contradictory, but stressing the vines produces better grapes. This is why Europeans, for centuries, have planted wine grapes where other crops struggle to survive—often on thin-soiled hillsides.[91] Growing grapes without supplying additional water after the rainy season is over is called dry farming. The Europeans who brought some of California's first vines also brought their grape-growing expertise. They introduced dry farming to the region, and it became a popular practice in California's earliest vineyards.

Dry farming is more of a soil tillage technique; it is the art of working the soil to create a sponge-like environment that causes the water to come up from below, into the sponge. Dry farmers seal the top of the soil with four to twelve inches of dry soil (referred to as "dust mulch"); this is made to act as a cap so that the moisture cannot rise to the top and evaporate. An added benefit of this "dust mulch" is that without moisture weeds cannot grow well in it, which minimizes the amount of weeding that is needed in the vineyard.[92] Speaking of soils, if the soil is sandy, water will drain through it quickly, and dry farming will not work well. Soil that is composed of loam or clay holds water better and is preferred. In Nevada County, the soil is more of a slow-draining type, which makes it perfect for dry farming. Locally, Sierra Starr Vineyard has an area in which they use dry farming successfully.[93]

In the later part of the 1800s, at a time when California was experiencing its first taste of worldwide wine acclaim, the winning wines from Sonoma and Napa were dry farmed. Some of the finest wines in the world are produced using dry-farmed fruit. The famous California wines that won the 1976 Paris Wine Tasting (the Judgment of Paris) were all dry farmed.[94] Today, California has dry-farmed vineyards all over the state, although, in total, they only amount to about 5 percent of all of California's vineyards, but that number is starting to increase.

Dry farming has a very long history. In the Mediterranean, grapes have been dry farmed for thousands of years. This method is not used to maximize yield; rather, it allows nature to dictate the true sustainability of the agricultural production in a particular region. Dry farming was an agricultural practice that allowed agricultural crops to be grown and cultivated on the prairie, which typically received low levels of rainfall and had very hot summers and harsh winters. There is evidence to suggest that Native Americans on the Great Plains and in the Southwest practiced dry farming. However, the European settlers in the region did not adopt this method until the late 1800s. Westward expansion necessitated the need to grow more food. The Homestead Act of 1862 granted settlers up to 160 acres of frontier land to cultivate or build on. By 1900, more than half a million families had settled in the West under the Homestead Act.[95]

Many people wonder how dry farming can possibly work. The simple answer is: science. By limiting the amount of water a plant gets, the fruit it produces will have an increased amount of sugar and other flavor compounds. This makes it easier to taste the fruit without all of the extra water in the way. Young grape vines are thirsty, so they go searching for water and send their roots deeper and deeper into the ground. This creates very sturdy vines; with heavy watering from above, vines have no reason to send their roots so deep. Shallow-rooted vines are not strong in high winds, and the loss of grapevines can be heartbreaking. Deep roots, combined with a top foot of soil, mean that moisture from below is prevented from coming to the top of the soil and evaporating away. Instead, the moisture stays below the surface.[96]

Spain has only recently loosened its regulations around irrigation, but it is still illegal in Europe's fine wine regions to water vineyards. The belief behind this is that watering the vineyards leads to a decreased quality in the region's wine.[97] In France, a natural delivery of water to their vineyards is essential to their terroir. They believe that terroir is the combination of natural forces that makes one vineyard site superior to another—even when they are adjacent. Terroir is a French term that, when translated, literally means "earth" or "soil." More loosely translated, terroir relates to how a particular region's climate, soil and aspect (terrain) affect the taste of its wine. Several elements combine to create a vineyard's terroir, including wind, temperature, humidity, degree and aspect of slope. But of all the elements that are important to terroir, water drainage is the most important.

DRIP IRRIGATION

The first drip irrigation systems were put into California vineyards in 1970, and dry farming was used less and less. There was a drought in 1976 and 1977 that led to more vineyards using drip irrigation systems. These systems conserved water, while they also allowed grape growers to regulate and control the amount of water their vines received. Their yields increased—plumper grapes meant more tons per acre—but the grapes held more water, which often diluted their flavor. Drip irrigation also caused roots to stay closer to the surface—these roots weren't deep enough to thrive in a California drought, through watering restrictions in the viticulture industry. Drip irrigation allowed growers to plant in new locations, including Australia, the most arid continent in the world. All of the wines that are now produced in Australia would not exist without drip irrigation.

But whether grape growers used dry farming or drip irrigation, premium wine producers restricted their yields in order to make superior products that they could sell for a higher price. Low-end wines need grapes from vineyards that produce ten to fifteen tons per acre. Some may wonder how grape growers can get that much more fruit per acre. By not restricting water and plumping out their grapes, these grape growers are able to increase their yields. If drought conditions continue to worsen in California, more growers will have to consider dry farming in order to keep their vineyards alive. Due to this possibility, there has been increased interest in dry farming among new vineyards. It is interesting to note that Northern California may be returning to more historic methods of grape production—similar to how it was done in the late 1800s in Nevada County. The grape vine is adaptable and, fortunately, drought-tolerant, so it is safe to assume that California will always be able to produce wine.

There are economic constraints with dry-farmed fruit. Although the fruit is sweeter, denser and easily stored, it is also smaller. The commercial fruit industry (including the wine grape industry) has spent many years working toward larger yields (with larger fruit). Dry farming is only viable if the wine produced is of a high enough quality to warrant a higher price. Dry-farmed vineyards reach production more slowly; it sometimes takes as long as five years for dry-farmed vineyards to start producing wine. But when they do, the quality of their fruits is very high.[98] While dry farming is not appropriate for every grape grower or every region in California, it is a promising system for crop management. It offers greater crop security in times when water is uncertain or threatened, and it can produce a higher-quality bottle of wine.

We know from history that dry farming does work in Western Nevada County, so reintroducing it to the area is less risky. Nevada County's rainfall is well above the minimum necessary for dry farming, fifteen to twenty inches per year. Dry farming not only requires sufficient rainfall, but it also requires moisture-retaining soils, which can be found in Nevada County. Dry farming is also beneficial because it keeps weeds from growing in vineyards.

Sierra Starr Vineyard, Nevada County's only local vineyard that uses dry farming methods. *Courtesy of Jackson Starr.*

The "dust mulch" (the dry layer of several inches of soil at the base of the vine) is dry enough to keep weeds from growing, which makes herbicides unnecessary. When less water is used for grape growing, the area's water supply and in-stream flows can experience a number of positive impacts. And when a vineyard practices dry farming, the energy used to transport and pump irrigation water to the vineyard is eliminated, and the need to install and maintain drip irrigation systems is eliminated. Perhaps the most exciting benefit of dry farming to a viticulturist is the better tasting and more densely nutritious fruit that is grown as a result.[99]

However, farming without irrigation has a major drawback: it dramatically reduces yields. But with grapes in particular, the grape skins contain flavor-making tannins and polyphenols, and dry farming can produce a higher proportion of skin material to juice, which results in richer, more intense wines.[100] One of the most serious issues facing the world today is the quality and quantity of water. The quality of the world's water, the water supply itself and the potential for significant drought, especially in California, are serious threats. Dry farming would certainly be a beneficial method for achieving many positive results, but most importantly, it would conserve water.

A YEAR IN THE VINEYARD

Many wonder what happens during each season in a vineyard. The Sierra Wine and Grape Growers Association has provided a summary of this process, which illustrates it well.[101]

Each season brings new chores and processes to ensure that the grapes in the vineyards are the best they can be. In spring, it's a busy time in the vineyard, and around February, after the worst of the winter rains have passed but before bud-break, it's time for the annual pruning chores. The timing (after most of the rains, before bud-break) is crucial to minimize the risk of over-wintering spores of fungi, which could infect open pruning wounds. The later a grape grower can postpone pruning, the faster the pruning wounds will heal. In the summertime, once the spring buds break into leaf, bloom occurs quickly. Zinc is often applied to the vine just before bloom, to help the vines "fruit set," encouraging large and full fruit clusters.

The vineyard's most dangerous enemy is not an insect or pest; rather, it is a fungus called powdery mildew. Well known to rose growers, powdery mildew spores overwinter on grapevine wood when the winter rains release them from their pods. Once the temperatures reach 50°F, this fungus multiplies and spreads rapidly. If left unchecked, powdery mildew attacks all of the grapevine—the wood, the leaves and the fruit—which weakens the vine and ruins the fruit. To prevent or combat this fungus or to keep it from growing, a fungicide must be sprayed on the vines. The most commonly used fungicide is a common organic compound: sulfur. With sulfur, there is no buildup, and it disappears in ten days. Most growers use a liquid form of sulfur mixed with water that they spray directly on the vines.

Summertime labor in the vineyards includes removing all of the extra shoots from the vines, with the exception of those from the buds selected in February. Limiting shoot growth and, therefore, fruit production ensures that each vine's energy is balanced between the shoot growth and fruit production, which leads to higher-quality fruit.

Autumn is a frenzy of activity in the vineyard that builds to a crescendo, and it is followed by a great sense of relief and reward. The grapes must remain on the vine to reach their targeted sugar levels. Water is usually withheld at this stage to concentrate the fruits' flavors as much as possible. Grape samples are picked and crushed every few days to check the fruit's sugar content with refractometers and hydrometers. Once the grapes reach the levels prescribed by the winery, harvest begins. Harvest is the end goal for every vineyard and is very exciting, but it is an exhausting time. When harvest begins, picking starts at daybreak and ends before noon to keep the grapes cool for perfect fermentation. It takes many hands to harvest grapes in a short amount of time. In the winter, it's time to let the grapevines, as well as the viticulturalists and winemakers, rest. The years are long and busy, and this rest allows for a review of the year, an analysis of the data and planning for the coming year.

Most grapes in Western Nevada County are grown at elevations between 1,000 and 2,500 feet. A higher percentage of these grapes grown are for red wine, and the warm days and cool nights produce some high-quality wines. A major drawback to growing grapes in Nevada County is the very limited pool of agricultural labor available. Labor can be found, but the skill levels may vary. This is why many vineyard owners maintain their vineyards themselves. They also look for contracts with wineries that include harvest and transport to the winery for production.[102]

Grafting is a fascinating process in which new grapevines are merged with existing and well-established rootstocks. There are many good reasons to use grafted vines. Rootstocks provide a number of benefits, including vigor control, tolerance to water stress and pest resistance. Nevada County does have phylloxera insect pests, and they can kill an entire vineyard that does not contain grafted vines (own-rooted, as it is also known).[103] It is important to remember to only use certified planting materials when planting a vineyard to be sure that it is "clean," or free of known viruses and pests.

9

Resurgence of the Wine Industry

Nevada County's local wine industry has gone through many cycles of success and failure, highs and lows and ups and downs since the days of the gold rush. Through it all, no one can argue that the land in western Nevada County was very well suited to growing wine grapes.

The very first vineyard of the current rebirth of the Nevada County wine industry came in 1974. A man named John Callendar planted Little Wolf Vineyard on Perimeter Road in the southern part of Nevada County, about eight miles from the community of Alta Sierra. On his seven-acre vineyard, he grew seven different red varietals, including cabernet sauvignon, pinot noir, charbono, petite sirah, grignolino, sereksia and zinfandel. Since Callendar did not have his own winery, the La Purisima Winery in Sunnyvale crushed the first commercial wine produced from his grapes.[104] The Callendar Vineyard was purchased in 1981 by Elizabeth and Richard Peterson of Newcastle, California. The grapes were grown, harvested and later crushed by Nevada City Cellars at their Rock Creek Winery, which was the county's only registered winery at that time.

Nevada City Cellars became Nevada City Winery and made arrangements with the City of Nevada City to have a vineyard and winery at the old airport site near Cement Hill. In the fall of 1982, Nevada City Cellars opened a "temporary" winery and retail sales outlet on Spring Street in Nevada City; it was located in the old foundry garage next to the American Victorian Museum (now the Miners Foundry Cultural Center). This location must

Foundry Garage, the location of Nevada City Winery. *Courtesy of Susie Bavo.*

have worked well for the Nevada City Winery, as they never moved to the airport location like they had planned.

In the 1980s, the new incarnation of the Nevada City Winery started producing wine. They sourced their grapes from regional vineyards, as they did not (and still do not) grow their own grapes. Once again, it became popular and fashionable for gentleman farmers to plant vineyards. This time, the vineyard renaissance was led by several men, including Bob Wilder, Pete Arnold, Dick Angel and Dr. Smith, Dr. Cobden and Dr. Jewett. These gentlemen were among the first to plant vineyards in Nevada County in the 1980s, which directly led to the growth of today's Nevada County wine industry.

Smith Winery was the second winery to open in Nevada County in 1987, and by 1991, there were five wineries in Nevada County. By the end of the twentieth century, there were six wineries in Nevada County.[105] Those six wineries were Nevada City Winery, Nevada County Wine Guild, Smith Vineyards and Winery, Indian Springs Vineyards, Double Oak Winery and Sierra Starr Winery.[106] Currently, Nevada County has thirteen wineries, but as more wineries open, sadly, some end up closing. The numbers seem to be ever changing; between 2018 and 2019 alone, Nevada County saw Smith, Solune, Coufos, Bent Metal and Sierra Knolls close their doors for various reasons—most often because the owners just wanted to retire.

SIERRA FOOTHILLS
AMERICAN VITICULTURAL AREA (AVA)

The Sierra Foothill region is known for its multitudes of microclimates, its granite and loam soils, its yearly average of forty-five to fifty-five inches of rainfall and its cool nights and warm days. As of this book's publication date, there are thirteen wineries operating in Nevada County, and they are all within the Sierra Foothills AVA (American Viticultural Area). The Sierra Foothills AVA, established in 1987, is one of the geographically largest AVAs in the country. It covers 2.6 million acres and contains portions of eight California counties: Amador, Calaveras, El Dorado, Mariposa, Nevada, Placer, Tuolumne and Yuba. Of the Sierra Foothills AVA's 2.6 million acres, 5,700 of them are planted with grapevines.[107] In total, there are eighty-three vineyards in the Sierra Foothills AVA, with a total planted area of 1,817 acres. This book, however, will only discuss the wineries in Nevada County.

SIERRA VINTNERS

Sierra Vintners is part of the Sierra Foothills American Viticultural Association (AVA), and it was established in 1987 on the western edge of the Sierra Nevada. This AVA is approximately 160 miles long and stretches from South Yuba County to Mariposa County; it also includes Nevada County. The wineries within the Sierra Vintners AVA produce a wide variety of vines and wines, with well over fifty varietals in Nevada County alone.[108] Nevada County's local grape growers and winemakers use premiere winemaking techniques to produce some of California's most delicious craft wines.

10

Local Wineries and their Histories

Nevada County is an amazing destination for day trips, weekend excursions and longer vacations. It features special hotels (both historic and modern), quaint and lovely bed-and-breakfasts, vacation rentals and even "glamping" opportunities—there's something for everyone. Add to that this area's excellent and plentiful restaurants and its art and culture, and it's clear why Nevada County is a true destination. The area also has wonderful history from the gold rush era, which just adds to the magic of Nevada County. Oh, and the wine. The awards that Nevada County's wines receive are very impressive for any wine region.

There is no other wine region like this one. The wines produced in Nevada County are many and varied. The people there are amazingly friendly, and visitors can often meet the owners and winemakers at the vineyards and tasting rooms. If visitors don't feel like venturing out to the wineries and vineyards, there are many lovely tasting rooms in both downtown Nevada City and Grass Valley to visit. These towns also contain many darling shops and art galleries. If visitors would rather spend their time at a winery that has its own vineyard, there are many vineyards with expansive, beautiful acres in which they can relax and enjoy the wine with a view…sometimes with a picnic lunch, live music or even a movie on the weekend.

Nevada County, California, has become a popular wine region that can easily compete with larger, more established wine regions, like Napa Valley and Sonoma Valley. Wineries in the Sierra Vintners appellation are similar to the wineries that were in Napa Valley forty years ago, when the owners and winemakers were easily accessible to visitors—sometimes, the owner is also the winemaker. The personal touch that is found in Nevada County is something that larger wineries often lose along the way. Nevada County's rich history, spectacular beauty, Mediterranean climate and smaller, more intimate experiences at the wineries and tasting rooms make it unique. Most of the time, visitors don't pay a tasting fee, and if they do, it is small and typically applied to their purchases. Of the thirteen wineries in Nevada County, no two are alike—their wines are all unique and delicious. The information that has been included for each winery was collected through a combination of personal interviews, email exchanges and promotional materials.

AVANGUARDIA WINERY

Avanguardia Winery blends over twenty Italian, Georgian, French and University of California (UC) patented grape varieties (crosses) from its vineyards to craft unique and prize-winning wines. In fact, many of the grape varieties grown at Avanguardia are not available anywhere else—outside of Europe.[109]

At Avanguardia, visitors won't find the typical California varietals, like cabernet, zinfandel or chardonnay. What they will find are wines that are different—wines that can't be found anywhere else in California. For example, their flagship white wine, cristallo, features a grape from the former Soviet Republic of Georgia. Their most unique red wine is called campio, and it is created by blending the UC-patented cross carmine with the northeast Italian refosco for a truly unique wine. At Avanguardia Wines, balance is of the utmost importance; their wines have just the right amount of alcohol, acidity, tannin and oak. Their wines avoid contemporary trends, and in many ways, their wines are more like European wines than typical Californian wines. By trying the range of more than nine proprietary blends, visitors can discover why they are on the cutting edge of craft blending.

Avanguardia Winery is a family business that was developed by Rob and Marilyn Chrisman, who both have family roots in farming. Rob's father's family came to California in the 1850s and ran a large produce ranch near what is now Ventura, California. Marilyn spent her youth roaming the wild country behind a small farm in Michigan. One of her fondest childhood memories happened when she was just six years old;

her father scooped up a handful of rich soil and told her to take a deep breath and smell the beauty of the earth. The historic Andres Personini Vineyard was located just down the road (Jones Bar Road) in Nevada City from Avanguardia. This property was rented in the early 1900s by Personini and was one of the earliest vineyards in Nevada County. This is not the location of the current Personini Ranch but is property that Andres acquired later.[110]

When Rob and Marilyn met in college in Los Angeles, they never expected to become farmers. However, they both rediscovered the joy of living in the country when Rob decided that he wanted to grow grapes and make wine. While he was in his twenties, Rob worked as a computer programmer and analyst and spent his lunch hours visiting stores, looking for vintage wines. He learned to appreciate the traditional blends of famous European wine regions. It was then that he also discovered that delicious grapes don't only come from France, but they also come from Italy, Spain and parts of eastern Europe. He was hooked. As he tasted and experimented, he set a goal for himself—he would make fine wines from grapes from around the world, which he would select for their blending potential to create unique flavor profiles. He wanted to build upon the traditional European approach; he wanted to blend grapes for flavor, acid balance and tannins for stability.

In 1977, Rob and Marilyn moved to the high foothills of Tulare County, where Rob planted and developed a small experimental vineyard. Rob had a degree in Slavic studies, but he taught himself viticulture and oenology—he still relied on expertise of others. Rob contacted the University of California at Davis (UC-Davis) Foundation Plant Services and worked with them to import new grape varieties to the United States. Rob Chrisman was one of the first U.S. vintners to import grape varieties from Italy that were previously unknown in the U.S. In 1990, Rob and Marilyn moved their growing family to Nevada County, where they captured the warm days and cool nights of the northern California foothills and started a commercial vineyard and winery. Today, you can find Rob either in the vineyard, tending the grapes, in the winery fine-tuning his unique blends or happily chatting with visitors who have come to enjoy his fine wines.

With a classic style in mind, Rob was able to creatively combine tradition and innovation. Historically, the European approach to wine is to blend fine, locally grown varietals to create great wines. Instead of only growing the French varieties of grapes that were traditionally grown in California, Rob chose different high-quality grapes from around the world. Each grape variety Rob chose was selected for its blending qualities of flavor, aroma, complexity, acid balance and tannins. For twelve years, he planted and experimented with viticulture and winemaking as a hobbyist. After contracting with University of California at Davis, their foundation plant materials department imported over a dozen Italian varieties for Rob—these were vines that, at that time, had never been grown before in the United States.

In 1990, after extensive soil and climate research, Rob selected the northern California foothills near Nevada City as the location of his commercial vineyard. Located in a mixed conifer forest, at an elevation of 2,100 feet, Rob chose to develop 3.5 acres of their 15-acre parcel into a vineyard and winery. It took a lot of work to clear the land, cross-rip the soil and clear rock. Rob's vines are irrigated by a carefully regulated drip system that uses sweet, clear well water. Rob also installed two trellis systems—each one matched the vigor of the grape variety. The two-armed lyre trellis was used for the vigorous sangiovese. And the more moderately vigorous vines, like semillon, were supported by a vertical shoot positioning trellis (VSP).

The terroir of a vineyard is that magical mix of climate, soil and water. The Avanguardia Vineyard has three different microsites—similar to regions in Italy. The southwest slope of Avanguardia is warm, dry and rocky, while the northeast slope is cooler with deeper soils. The bottomland near the stream is cool, but rocky. The vineyard's soil is clay loam, and its temperatures peak in the low nineties in the summer—they are moderated by frequent

Avanguardia Vineyard in autumn. *Courtesy of Rob Chrisman.*

Delta breezes from the coast. Spring and fall are often very long and mild, and the winter usually brings two or three snowstorms, with temperatures that occasionally fall into the twenties. The vineyard's average yearly rainfall is between fifty-five and seventy inches, and most of it falls in the wintertime. By understanding the different microsites of his vineyard, Rob is able to plant the grape varieties that are most closely matched with ideal growing conditions. The varieties he grows are so unique that they cannot be found in many places outside of Italy.

Rob Chrisman getting ready to plant a grapevine in a hole he just dug. *Courtesy of Marilyn Chrisman.*

Rob plants the heat-loving grape varieties (sangiovese, negrara and barbera) high on the southwest slope. Rkatsiteli, with its Georgian winter heritage, buds at the end of May, and Rob plants it at the bottom of the southwest slope, where the frosts persist. The southwest slope also has a small section of corvina and molinara grapes. Short season whites (melon de bourgogne, pinot blanc and pinot gris) are grown on the uppermost northeast slope. In addition to these white grapes, the northeast slope also has rows of corvina, carmine, mondeuse, biancolella, erbaluce, forastera, tocai friulano, flora and semillon. The bottomland is planted with dolcetto, rondinella, montepulciano, chenin blanc, perverella and orange muscat.

Veraison (coloring of the grapes) typically happens in July and August. Grape clusters are thinned to yield the goal of three and a half tons per acre. After veraison, watering is often limited to create more flavorful fruit. Harvest season can stretch from the end of August to the middle of November, depending on the grape variety and weather conditions. To determine a vine's ripeness, Rob checks berry samples of each variety for brix, pH, total acidity and condition, and Marilyn checks the seeds and skins for color and taste. This boutique winery produces between 750 and 1,000 cases of delicious premium blends each year. In 2006, Rob and Marilyn Chrisman opened their winery and tasting room to the public.

LUCCHESI VINEYARDS AND WINERY

High on a hillside that overlooks Nevada County, with breathtaking views of the Sierra Nevada mountain range, is Lucchesi Vineyards and Winery. Owners Mario and Linda Clough planted the vineyard in 1999 and opened the winery in 2002. Lucchesi's grapes are grown on twenty acres of steeply terraced vineyards called the View Forever Vineyard. The vineyard is very appropriately named, as the views there are spectacular. The vineyard has a southwest exposure to maximize the sun's rays; this perfectly ripens the grapes and perfects the balance of concentrated flavors, color and texture. Lucchesi Vineyards and Winery specializes in traditionally crafted wines that are produced in small lots in order to capture their varietal characters and regional qualities. This small family-owned vineyard and winery is the pride and joy of Mario and Linda Clough. Most days, Mario can be found working in the vineyard, and Linda can be found hosting visitors and pouring wine to taste, either at the vineyard (by appointment) or at the downtown Grass Valley tasting room at 128 Mill Street.

So where does the name Lucchesi actually come from? Mario's birth surname was Lucchesi. His father was a chemist, and he became a part owner of a detergent factory in La Paz, Bolivia, after he grew tired of ranching in Argentina. He purchased a gold mine in the Andes Mountains with a partner, and while he was on an expedition to locate the mine, he was killed by a stray bullet. Since the nearest doctor was a three-day ride in each direction, Mario's father did not survive. Mario was named after his Uncle Mario—his father's brother—who took care of his mother, Sarita, his sister, Silvia, and him after his father died. Uncle Mario owned a hotel near the airport, where he hired his sister-in-law (Mario's mother). While working there, she met an American named Forest Lynn Clough. He was a bush pilot who flew geologists and supplies around the Amazon and Andes. They were eventually married, and Forest Clough adopted Mario and his sister. They later moved to the United States and changed their names from Mario and Silvia Lucchesi to Mario and Silvia Clough. In honor of his family, Mario and Linda decided to name their vineyard and winery Lucchesi.

The roots of the Lucchesi family lie in Provincia Di Lucca, Toscana. The Lucchesis are direct descendants of the civilizations of the Etruscans, the native culture of northwestern and central Italy. The Etruscan civilization was also the first of Italy and the Romans.[111] Lucca was a major Etruscan city of Etruria (ancient Toscana), and its name, Lucchesi, is derived from

The "View Forever" at Lucchesi Vineyard. *Courtesy of Mario Clough.*

Mario Clough, the co-owner (with wife Linda) of Lucchesi Winery and Vineyards, sits and appreciates his wine and his winery's beautiful setting. *Author photograph.*

109

the ancient Etruscan word *luk*, which means "lake." Later, the Romans, who were native to west-central Italy, conquered the entire Italian Peninsula, and Lucca became a Roman colony. Mario's family left Italy in the late 1930s to escape the oppression of Mussolini, and they moved to Egypt in North Africa. As the Nazi forces gradually took over the region, his family moved to South America.

The View Forever Vineyard, as Mario calls it, is built on twenty terraced acres in a beautiful setting, where visitors can, almost literally, see forever. The land was once part of the Wheeler Ranch.[112] When Mario and Linda bought the property, the views were hidden by trees and brush, but they had faith that the view was there—they were absolutely right.

Mario and his crew took great care when selecting the grape varieties to plant. They paired different grapes to ensure that the type of soil and amount of sunlight were the best fits for each varietal. Lucchesi Vineyards and Winery produces three white wines: chardonnay, pinot grigo and sauvignon blanc. Their red wines include cabernet franc, cabernet sauvignon, petite sirah, tempranillo, merlot, sangiovese, syrah, zinfandel, a red blend and a port.[113] In addition to its vineyard and tasting room on View Forever Lane, Lucchesi Vineyards and Winery has a beautiful and spacious tasting room on Mill Street in downtown Grass Valley. Visitors can enjoy live music while sipping their delicious wines on most weekends.

GRAY PINE VINEYARD AND WINERY

Gray Pine Vineyard and Winery was named for the native California Gray Pine trees that are common in this area. Located in Penn Valley on Branding Iron Road (close to the corner of Pleasant Valley Drive and Highway 20), this small, limited-production winery has an annual production of approximately 350 cases. Their grapes are grown on a two-acre vineyard that was planted by owner and winemaker Guy Lauterbach. Everything at Gray Pine Winery is estate-grown (which means that they only make their wines from the grapes they grow in their vineyard). Gray Pine produced their first wine as a commercial winery in 2011. Gray Pine specializes in Bordeaux varietals, and they produce cabernet sauvignon, merlot, cabernet franc, petit verdot, malbec and a classic Boudreaux-style red blend. They also produce a very small amount of sauvignon blanc.[114]

Gray Pine Vineyard in Penn Valley. *Author photograph.*

A grape crusher (*left*) with a beautiful vineyard view at Gray Pine Vineyard and Winery. *Author photograph.*

Gray Pine's winemaking focus is on food-friendly wines with balanced acids and tannins that are created in the classic Bordeaux style. Guy Lauterbach, a self-described lifelong wine aficionado, is a retired computer industry engineer. Not long after the 49er fire ripped through Penn Valley in September 1988, while he was living in the Bay Area in the 1990s, Lauterbach purchased his vineyard's land. He moved there in 2001 and planted his two-acre vineyard in 2008. His first vintage was released in 2011, and he hasn't looked back since. He prefers wines with an old-world slant, higher acidity, less jammy fruit and minimal oak. Guy greets visitors in his onsite tasting room, and he enjoys telling stories and sharing his wines.[115]

PILOT PEAK WINERY

Established in early 2004, Pilot Peak Winery was constructed from a converted metal shop building. In its first year of operation, the winery produced 600 cases of wine that later sold out in record time. The winery currently produces about 2,500 cases of wine each year, and it has been fortunate to win many gold medals, including Best of Show and Best of Class awards from the state fair and the *San Francisco Chronicle*. Len and Nancy Stevens and Lynn and Jacque Wilson opened the winery, but its new owners, Mike and Vanessa Colomb, purchased the Wilsons' share in 2018.[116] They are all hands-on owners and are hosts to their visitors.

Pilot Peak Winery is located in Penn Valley in a lovely setting that is peaceful and relaxing. It has a winery, a tasting room and several terraces under some trees, where its guests can sit back and enjoy the wine and small plate appetizers it offers. The winery itself is a cedar and stone building that reflects the rustic charm of the Gold Country. In the winery's traditional tasting room, visitors can taste its estate-grown sauvignon blanc and mourvedre. Visitors can also sample the winery's other wines (barbera, chardonnay, sparkling cuvee brut, cabernet franc, petite sirah, syrah, tempranillo and their red blend ZaMORE) that are made from grapes sourced within a five-mile radius of the winery. From picking the grapes, to fermentation and onsite bottling, Pilot Peak's wine is truly hand crafted.[117]

The owners of Pilot Peak believe that food and wine should be enjoyed together—with friends and family—and that is why they offer a complimentary "Comparative Wine Tasting" of their award-winning wines.

Springtime at Pilot Peak Winery. *Courtesy of Pilot Peak Winery.*

These tastings are served in **flights of four** (in numbered glasses) so visitors can compare and contrast each one. Appetizers are served with the wine so patrons can appreciate the **marriage of food** and wine.[118]

Early settlers often used Pilot Peak (the hill, not the winery) as a navigation aid—a point of reference. The sixty-two-acre property of Pilot Peak Winery and Vineyard was purchased from the Brown family in 2001. This was just a small portion of the Brown Ranch, which was once a large dairy farm in the 1900s. It has since become a large cattle ranch that still operates next to Pilot Peak Winery. In fact, the winery is surrounded by large cattle ranches on all sides, making it very beautiful and peaceful.[119]

NEVADA COUNTY WINE GUILD

The Nevada County Wine Guild has been commercially making wine for more than thirty years, and it has been making wine organically for the past twenty years—this makes them a bit unique in Nevada County. They also have the highest production rate and widest distribution radius of all the wineries in Nevada County, with their wines sold nationwide.

Tony Norskog is a partner and the winemaker for the Nevada County Wine Guild. He received his degree in enology from UC Davis (a very prestigious winemaking school) in 1977. He has been making wines for over twenty-five years—first as head winemaker for Nevada City Winery. His vast life experiences include many adventures through California's Central Coast and time spent in France as chief tank washer and grape crusher. It's safe

Nevada County Wine Guild's "Our Daily Cab." *Courtesy of Nevada County Wine Guild.*

to say that Tony has done it all when it comes to winemaking. Tony has also been at the forefront in the organic wine world, helping to create excellent wine that is not only organic but sulfite-free and fairly priced. It was (and still is) important to Tony that he makes wine in a more environmentally friendly way. He wants his children to be able to run through the vineyard without being exposed to any harmful chemicals.

Donn Berdahl, Tony's assistant winemaker and partner, joined the winery in 2004. Donn was the former general manager and on-site winemaker for a large custom crush facility that processed grapes for many well-known wineries and growers. Together, Tony and Donn have been on a purposeful mission of crafting delicious wines conscientiously—but without pretense. Donn and Tony's synergy has resulted in the company's tremendous growth. It has become a national brand that distributes wine to nearly every state in the United States.[120] Our Daily Red is perhaps their most well-known wine; it is a blend of syrah, grenache, ruby cabernet and carignan. They primarily make their wines from grapes grown in the Central Valley of California. They also offer Our Daily Cab, which is a single varietal Cabernet Sauvignon. Both wines have no detectable sulfites; they are also gluten free, vegan and certified USDA organic—all for around $11 a bottle.

SIERRA STARR

Visitors can see the Sierra Starr vineyards as they leave Grass Valley on Highway 20. Before relocating to Grass Valley, the Starrs owned Elkhorn Farms in Monterey County, where they grew and provided specialty flowers for over twenty years.[121] The Starrs bought the existing vineyard when they moved to Nevada County in 1995. They moved with the intent of also moving their floral nursery from the Monterey Bay to the vacant land on the parcel. Phil has always been a farmer at heart, so when they decided to not move the nursery, Phil was challenged and intrigued by the idea of growing grapes and making fine wine. Anyone who knows Phil Starr knows that once he sets his mind on something, it can become all-consuming. The hard work of both Phil and Anne Starr has created a beautiful vineyard, winery and lovely tasting room in the heart of downtown Grass Valley.[122]

In 2005, Phil and Anne's son, Jackson, joined the family business. He is the vineyard manager and assistant winemaker, and he is also a wine judge and certified sommelier. Phil is very hands-on with the vineyard and winery, and Anne operates the downtown Grass Valley tasting room and Sirius Sipper wine club.[123]

The Sierra Starr tasting room is located in downtown Grass Valley at the clock tower. Its building was constructed in 1870, and the Starr family has done a remarkable job in restoring it and creating a beautifully warm and welcoming tasting room and gift shop in it. One wall displays the original red brick, and the opposite wall was made from mine rock that came from local gold mines more than 140 years ago—it has all been hand restored. Phil Starr hand crafted the beautiful custom bar. Visitors should take notice of the hand-painted mural that illustrates the Starrs' vineyards and winery. They should also note the hand-carved tasting room door—both were created by local artist Rainn.

When asked whether they used any dry-farming methods at Sierra Starr, Jackson Starr replied:

> *Yes, we do dry farm some of our petite sirah. Basically, what it means is that we do not irrigate the vines. They survive simply on the rainfall that we get during the rainy season. The vines have to develop deep root systems to seek out the water. These vines are strong, hardy, balanced and produce less fruit. The fruit that we harvest from these vines are intense and concentrated. We wish we could do more dry farming, but in early trials, the vines on the top of our hillsides seem to be too far from a ground water source. I do, however, see us attempting more dry farming in the future.[124]*

The original vineyard was first planted in 1979 and 1980, and the original vineyard consisted of five acres of sauvignon blanc, cabernet sauvignon and zinfandel. In the summer of 1998, an additional acre of cab franc was planted. In the summer of 2000, an entire zinfandel vineyard was planted using scion (fruiting) wood that was brought in from the Ciapusci Vineyard, a one-hundred-year-old vineyard located in Mendocino County. In 2006 and 2007, an additional planting of cabernet franc and new plantings of petite sirah and alicante bouchete were added to the vineyard. The Sierra Starr Vineyard now holds twelve acres of grapes from which they make most of their award-winning wines. Construction of their completely submerged, gravity flow winery was completed in 2010. This new structure gave them more space and the means to craft even better wines more efficiently.

Unique to Sierra Starr winery is the addition of a concrete egg that is used for winemaking. Several years ago, Phil and Anne were touring wineries in Virginia, when they came upon a winery that used a concrete egg to make sauvignon blanc. Phil didn't forget that wine, because he really liked it—it was

Above: Phil Starr giving a vineyard tour at Sierra Starr Vineyards and Winery. *Author photograph.*

Opposite: Phil Starr pouring wine into his concrete egg at Sierra Starr Winery. *Jackson Starr.*

different from any other sauvignon blanc he had tasted.[125] Around the same time, Jackson Starr discovered wines that a few other foothill winemakers in Calaveras County and Amador County were producing using concrete eggs. The benefit of a concrete egg is that it enriches a wine's texture and flavor, and it is durable and easy to clean. Just before the harvest of 2016, the Starrs purchased their own concrete egg; they then set it up to ferment their sauvignon blanc. For the Starrs, the egg also fit with their goal to reduce energy consumption at the winery. The concrete egg needs no heating or cooling beyond the ambient temperature of their winery, which was built into a hillside and kept naturally cool. A bank of fifty-six solar panels was also installed, and since they are experimenting with dry farming in part of their vineyard, the Starrs rely on only the rains each winter to keep the vines flourishing and the fruit of highest quality.

SZABO VINEYARDS

The roots of the Szabo family lie in the town of Eger, Hungary, where vineyards have existed since the days of the Romans. The Szabos have a love of (and a genetic predisposition for) full-throttled, robust red wines, and this love led Sandor (also known as Alex) Szabo to appreciate the finest European wines. His desire to produce only the best quality grapes (and, ultimately, the best quality wine) was the result of all these things.[126]

After extensively researching where to locate his vineyard, Alex was led to explore locations from Washington State to San Luis Obispo, California. He ultimately chose the Grass Valley and Nevada City region for Szabo Vineyards. They were convinced that many of the best zinfandels were made using Sierra Foothill grapes, and historically, some of the first vineyards in California were located in the Sierra Foothills at the time of the gold rush. There, they found the texture of the soils to be extremely rocky, well-draining and slightly acidic—perfect for their forty-acre vineyard in the Bitney Springs area of Nevada City.[127]

Alex Szabo strives to work in harmony with nature and to protect the environment, and he also strives to produce the highest quality grapes in his vineyard. Sustainable farming practices have enabled the vineyard to keep pesticide use to a minimum and has stopped soil erosion. Sustainable wine growing practices help reduce water and energy consumption, minimize the use of pesticides, build healthy soils, recycle natural resources, protect

Szabo Vineyards. *Courtesy of Szabo Vineyards.*

air quality and maintain the surrounding wildlife habitat. Alex Szabo was awarded the 2004 Conservationist of the Year award by the National Conservation Resource Services of Nevada County.[128]

All of the wines produced by Szabo are made exclusively from their own estate-grown grapes, which are known for being big, bold and fruit-forward. They are proud of the quality of their fruit and how it is fully expressed in the hand-crafted quality of their wines. Szabo's forty-acre vineyard operates at an elevation of 1,900, and it sits almost halfway between Nevada City and Grass Valley. The views are beautiful of the Pacific Coastal Range, Sutter Buttes and Sierra Buttes.

Szabo uses canopy management techniques in the vineyard in order to achieve balanced vines; with this technique, the winery can actively manage the micro-climate of the fruiting zone, which significantly increases the quality of its fruit. Located on the northeastern section of the estate's hillside, the winery's state-of-the-art, passive solar panels are built into the hillside and engineered to keep the wines at a constant temperature year-round. Szabo's offerings include sauvignon blanc, a dessert muscat as well as an off dry muscat, grenache, zinfandel, primitivo, syrah, petite sirah, and a rhone blend named viola.

NAGGIAR VINEYARDS

After Mike Naggiar retired from his thirty-two-year career with Hewlett Packard, he was looking for a second chapter and wanted something challenging. He took his passion for his family's single-acre hobby vineyard in Saratoga, California, and, along with his wife, Diane, began an extensive search throughout Northern California for a suitable location for a commercial vineyard. It took three years of searching for the perfect location, but Mike and Diane finally found sixty acres of land just southwest of Grass Valley. In 1998, with the help of an expert in vineyard construction and planting, the couple planted their first Nevada County vines and began learning the business of grape growing. It wasn't long before they were selling premium wine grapes and gaining a superior reputation among the most discriminating winemakers in Napa, Sonoma and the Sierra Foothills. What started as one retired couple's new adventure quickly turned into a true family business. Mike Naggiar is happiest when he is growing something, so he regularly tends to the vineyard while others make the wine. The Naggiars' vines start growing in January and are harvested during the night around September.[129]

The Naggiars' family members and friends were drawn to the beautiful and serene vineyard setting that they had created, and it was around a full dinner table that the idea of making their own wines came about. With more than seventeen varietals growing on their vineyard and over six years of experience with growing premium grapes, the Naggiars decided that it was the right time to take the next logical step in their adventure. The influx of family members to the Naggiar estate began. First, Mike's nephew Tony Tibshirani, his wife, Linda, and their family moved down from Montreal, Canada, and settled on an adjacent piece of land in 2001. Mike and Diane's only son, Shawn Naggiar, his wife, Mary, and their young family soon followed, expanding the family holdings and adding to the available workforce. Shawn and Mary built their home in the vineyards in 2008. At that point, each family member had a place in the family business.[130]

As the Naggiars' wines grew in personality and popularity, the family decided that the tastings they hosted "by appointment only" in their living room were no longer adequate. In 2009, the Naggiar family broke ground to build a more formal (and stunningly beautiful) 3,500-square-foot Tuscan-style tasting room that has since become a well-known destination for locals and out-of-town visitors alike. The tasting room hosts live music on Friday and Saturday nights and a Winefest summer concert series, and it has a bistro that serves delicious gourmet Mediterranean dishes for lunch and dinner—all in a picturesque setting. Combined, this makes Naggiar a jewel in the Nevada County winery crown.

Eighteen estate-grown varietals in four distinct categories of grapes are grown at Naggiar: Rhone, Italian, Bordeaux and Spanish. The Rhone varieties include viognier, marsanne, roussane, grenach, syrah, mourvedre, petit sirah, cinsault and counoise. Italian varieties include muscat canelli, sangiovese, barbera and primativo. Bourdeaux varieties include malbec,

The beautiful grounds at Naggiar Vineyards and Winery. *Author photograph.*

Mike Naggiar explaining how grapes are grown to a tour group. *Author photograph.*

cabernet sauvignon, cabernet franc and petit verdot. The only Spanish variety at Naggier is tempranillo. While each varietal makes a great bottle of wine, several fine blends and reserve wines are crafted by combining some of the varietals above.[131] Although their vineyard was started on 60 acres in 1998, the Naggiars have acquired additional land to increase their operation to 135 acres. The family lives on the vineyard, as it is truly a family operation.

MONTOLIVA VINEYARD AND WINERY

The community of Chicago Park, which is just a few miles from Grass Valley, was originally settled in the mid-1880s by German and Italian Americans. These immigrants came to Northern California to look for good locations for their vineyards and orchards. At one time, the Rolph and Bierwagen families owned much of what is now called Chicago Park. None of the original vineyards still exist there, but Chicago Park is still an agricultural epicenter in Nevada County.

A newer vineyard and winery in Chicago Park is Montoliva Vineyard and Winery. Montoliva is Italian for "Mount Olive," which is the name of the road where the winery is located. Founded in 2000, Montoliva Vineyard and Winery creates Tuscan-inspired wines of uncommon depth and character. Mark and Julianne Henry own the vineyard, and Mark is also the vineyard's manager and winemaker. They are both proud of the way that their winery reflects the spirit of their pioneering forebearers. With warm summers, cool evenings and soils of decomposed granite, Montoliva's location is nearly perfect for the central and southern Italian varietals that Mark loves to grow.[132]

Montoliva's estate varitals of sangiovese, moscato and aglianico were planted in 2000. At the same time, Vivai Cooperative Rauscedo, Italy's largest grapevine nursery, opened a subsidiary in California, and, for the first time, many prized sangiovese clones were available. Montoliva vineyard has more clonal diversity than any other sangiovese vineyard in all of California. Since planting his first vine in 2000, Mark has added teroldego, montepulciano and aleatico to his sangiovese, aglinico and moscato, making Montoliva the most focused producer of estate-grown Italian varietals in the northern Sierra Foothills.[133]

Montoliva's wines are made in the complex, masculine style of Tuscany. Mark Henry believes that long, slow fermentations using special Tuscan

Although the vineyard is usually below the snow line, snowstorms still occur. This is a photograph of Montoliva in the snow. *Courtesy of Mark Henry.*

yeasts, extended macerations and barrel aging all contribute to the strengths of sangiovese and aglianico grapes. Henry also believes that small, family-operated vineyards and wineries—like Montoliva—can provide an agricultural experience that makes Nevada County stand out from the crowd.[134]

In addition to sangiovese and aglianico, Montoliva's current offerings include single varietal nebbiolo, teroldego, negroamaro, falanghina, primitivo, barbera and pinot grigio. The vineyard's wines are aged in a combination of new and old French and Slovakian barrels, which allow them to blend and create wines that are "muscular, deep, complex and, yet, still soft to the touch." Most of their wines are aged for twenty-four months before they are bottled, and the reserve bottlings age for a minimum of three years in the barrel.[135]

According to Mark Henry,

> *This area was* [home] *to an offshoot of the Maidu tribe of indigenous people, mainly because it is mostly below the snow line and because of its proximity to the Bear River. During the time of westward expansion,*

the Donner Trail ran right through the middle of my vineyard (according to the USGS). From the gold rush era, all the way up through the 1960s, this property, and most of the surrounding property, was owned by the Rolph family [German by way of England]. *The area around Montoliva Vineyard was used for orcharding and livestock, especially livestock, because there is an underground spring that comes up on the property and feeds the intermittent creek that separates the North Vineyard from the South Vineyard. The original foundation that my home sits on dates from the early twentieth century (not so sure how it will do in an earthquake). Most of the land around the current Chicago Park School, including the school property itself (which was donated to the community by the Rolph family), was parceled off in the 1970s. The property had a couple of different owners before I purchased it in 2000.*[136]

I planted the North Vineyard in sangiovese and aglianico in 2001. The south Vineyard was planted in primitivo, negroamaro, montepulciano and teroldego in 2015. In 2016, the east Vineyard (directly behind the school) was planted in aleatico and canaiolo nero. It may also be of interest to you that the old Belle Haven Orchard on Wabash (if you are driving from my place to [Grass Valley], *just past the Happy Apple Kitchen, the gravel road that goes straight at the ninety-degree turn) is in the process of being converted into commercial vineyard. In 2016, we planted an acre each of nero d'avola, teroldego and aglianico. In 2017, we planted an acre of aglianico. In 2020, we are planting a half acre each of falanghina and vermentino and an acre of barbera. Except for the teroldego and barbera, all the varietals I have planted here and on Wabash are southern Italian varietals.*[137]

Montoliva's wines win awards, and even though it is a relatively small vineyard (producing 1,500 cases per year), it is very well respected and highly awarded.

DOUBLE OAK VINEYARDS AND WINERY

Close to Highway 20, fifteen miles north of Nevada City and not far from the North San Juan Ridge, visitors will find Double Oak Vineyards and Winery. This winery is located at an elevation of 2,500 feet, which is the higher end of the elevation range of the Sierra Foothills appellation. At one time, this land was home to a cattle ranch, but by the 1970s, it had been subdivided and had quickly become overgrown and neglected. Bob and Ginny Hilsman homesteaded the property's original ten acres, started a family, made cheese, raised goats and grew a large garden for about a decade before deciding to plant grapes in 1982.[138] Bob and Ginny had a lot of hard work to do to clear the land (now fifty acres) and create the beautiful, environmentally sustainable vineyard that it is today.

At Double Oak, visitors will feel the serenity of being in a beautiful stand of native woodland of oaks, pines and madrones as they taste award-winning wines that were made by people who truly love what they do. Ginny and Bob Hilsman have been growing wine grapes on nine acres of mountain vineyards since 1982. Their first harvest was in 1985, and their first vintage was released in 1986.[139]

Double Oak wines display the intensity of mountain-grown fruit, which is full-bodied, yet, well balanced and complex. Accessible when first released, Double Oak's well-structured tannins also allow the vineyard's wines to bottle age well. The vineyard barrel ages its red wines for twenty-three months and

Double Oak Vineyard. *Author photograph.*

then it bottle ages them for another six months before they are released. Many things can be credited with the high quality of Double Oak's wine, including the vineyard's location (terroir) and its sustainable farming and winemaking practices. Double Oak is committed to sustainable and nature-friendly practices, from the vineyard to the winery.[140]

All of Double Oak's handcrafted wines are made from estate-grown, fully ripened and hand-harvested fruit. Since the vineyard is located in a slightly higher elevation than most other western Nevada County vineyards, it has a slower ripening season, which creates an ideal sugar and acid balance. When the sugars and flavors are just right, the vineyard harvests its grapes by hand. To protect the grapes from midday heat, the vineyard harvests early in the day.

Double Oak Winery produces a nice variety of red wines, including zinfandel, merlot, cabernet sauvignon and a late harvest zinfandel. For a balanced offering, it also produces a rosé and chardonnay. A trip to the vineyard's winery and tasting room is enjoyable as well as very educational, as Bob and Ginny love to share their over forty years of grape growing and winemaking experience. Visitors should tour the winery, walk in the vineyards and just enjoy wine at this delightful family farm and artisan winery.

NEVADA CITY WINERY

Nevada City Winery is the largest and oldest winery in Nevada County. It was also the first bonded winery that was opened in Nevada County after Prohibition ended. The winery represents the rustic history and elegance of Nevada County's wine region. As the oldest operating winery in the area, Nevada City Winery's founder, Allan Haley, and its winemaker, Tony Norskog, were given credit for revitalizing the wine industry in the 1980s in this region.[141]

Founded in a garage as Snow Mountain Winery in 1980, the business started booming. It quickly moved to the Miners Foundry garage in 1982, and it still stands there today. The original Nevada City Winery was founded in the late 1800s on Spring Street, just two blocks up the street, behind the National Exchange Hotel. In 1885, the original Nevada City Winery produced 5,000 cases of wine from local grapes. In 1990, it was estimated that Nevada City Winery sold 8,000 cases per year, and in 1998, production was estimated at 9,000 cases annually. Nevada City Winery has

Miners Foundry garage, where the Nevada City Winery resides today. *Author photograph.*

no vineyard, so it has no estate-bottled wines. However, Nevada City Winery has purchased grapes from local growers to produce award-winning wines since 1980. Local winemakers Tony Norskog and Mark Foster were also very important in getting a resurgence to take hold in Nevada County's wine industry. Today, Mark Foster is still the head winemaker at Nevada City Winery, and Tony Norskog is the owner and winemaker of the Nevada County Wine Guild.[142]

Nestled in historic downtown Nevada City, this winery's structure rests between the same brick buildings and Victorian houses that were built by miners during the gold rush of 1849. The winery's current location at 321 Spring Street was meant to only be a temporary tasting room and winery—however, the facility worked so well that they never relocated. The winery's winemaking operation and tasting room share the same building, so it is convenient to get a winery tour while enjoying their wines. They are open for tasting daily, which is also unique to the region, but their size enables them to employ the staff they need to offer tastings daily—except for major holidays.

Nevada City Winery's large tasting room. *Courtesy of Kim Crevoiserat.*

Nevada City wines in the cup of a Pelton Wheel. *Courtesy of Kim Crevoiserat.*

Nevada City Winery has twenty-seven wines in its portfolio, and it continues to produce new vintages each year. The wines produced by Nevada City Winery have won hundreds of awards, and the winery produces many varietals and blends. The winery's white wines include gewurztraminer, sonata (a blend), viogner, chardonnay and sauvignon blanc. Rosés include tempranillo rosé and alpenglow (a blend). As for red wines, they produce merlot, barbera, syrah, petite sirah, Rough And Ready red (a blend), grenache, cabernet sauvignon, dolcetto, petit verdot, solaire (a blend), cabernet franc, primativo, zinfandel, sangiovese and pinot noir. Their NV Dulcinea (a blend of five traditional Portuguese varietals) is their dessert wine. This astounding variety of wines has made Nevada City Winery not only the oldest, but also the largest winery in western Nevada County.[143] In addition to its beautiful tasting room and gift shop, the Nevada City Winery often hosts artists in their art gallery. Different artists are featured each month, and it is open to the public, free of charge.

TRUCKEE RIVER WINERY

The Truckee River Winery was established in 1989, and its owners had a vision of sourcing high-quality grapes to make delicious wines in Truckee. The winery's high elevation and cold temperatures naturally cool the fermentation and slow down the barrel aging process. Truckee River Winery is known as the "highest and coldest winery," and because of this, growing grapes is not an option.

Russ and Joan Jones, the owners of Truckee River Winery, started making wine in their two-car garage in Sierra Meadows, a suburb of Truckee. For nine years, Russ and Joan made great wine for their family members and friends in the area. The responses to their wines were so good that they decided to expand to become a commercial winery. The couple moved the winery from their garage into a two-story barn on the Truckee River. There, Russ, with the help of his daughter and friends, was able to expand production to 2,500 cases. In 2010, the couple opened a tasting facility, where locals and visitors could come and enjoy their wines—the fruit of their hard work.[144] The winery is truly a family-owned and -operated business in the heart of the coldest town in America. Russ and Joan lovingly refer to their winery as the "Highest and Coldest and Snowiest." Russ Jones is the winemaking director, and

Left: Russ Jones, the owner of Truckee River Winery, pressing grapes in the late 1990s. *Courtesy of Truckee River Winery.*

Below: Exterior of the Truckee River Winery with seating and bocce courts. *Author photograph.*

he makes all of their red wines. The Joneses' daughter, Katy Carroll Jones, is the general manager and white wine maker.

Since the beginning, the Joneses' focus has been to produce handcrafted wines with great structure and finesse. Their award-winning pinot noir is the winemakers' pride and joy. Since 2005, their wines have consistently won awards from the *San Francisco Chronicle* Wine Competition. The wines they produce include pinot gris, chardonnay, symphony, rosé, red barn red, merlot, zinfandel, pinot noir, malbec and apres (a dessert wine). Truckee River Winery continues to be a fun, high quality winery dedicated to preserving the local environment and providing a quality product for locals and tourists alike.

Truckee, California, is a historic town that is most noted as being a true Wild West railroad town. It is immersed in Native American history, pioneer history and gold rush history. The Truckee Winery itself is located in a historic part of town that was once the China Village (or Chinatown) for railroad workers. More recently, the tasting room building and surrounding areas were home to a cattle ranch in the early 1960s before the highway and bypass was built.[145] The Truckee River Winery not only makes excellent wines, but it also offers a nice selection of local beers, food (including tapas and artisan deli items), bocce ball courts and many other outdoor games. It is also dog friendly and is a wonderful place to spend some time with friends.

CLAVEY VINEYARDS AND WINERY

Tucked in the Sierra Foothills, not far from the Yuba and Bear Rivers, is a family-owned boutique winery called Clavey Vineyards and Winery. At Clavey, they use sustainable winemaking methods to bring the fullest expression of flavor in every single glass. The winery's selection of flavorful award-winning wines celebrates nature with every sip. The Clavey wines include oaked chardonnay, sangiovese, rosé, syrah, merlot, cabernet sauvignon, syrah and zinfandel. All of their wines are vegan-friendly, which means that they don't introduce any animal by-products into their wines or vines. The wines are also free of additives and chemicals; they undergo minimal processing, which means they have lower levels of sulfites and a lot of antioxidants. Their fresh and vibrant flavors are appreciated by many, and if visitors are sensitive to sulfites or want certified vegan wine, Clavey is an excellent choice.[146]

Originally established by Marc Orman, Clavey Vineyards and Winery is named after Clavey Falls, a class-five rapid on the Tuolumne River, near Yosemite. While rafting down Clavey Falls, Marc and his brother, Rodger, had a life-threatening experience when their raft flipped unexpectedly. As a lifelong whitewater adventurer, Marc didn't expect the near-death experience. It left him and his brother stranded without food or supplies, but it changed his outlook on life. Feeling lucky to have lived through the experience, Marc wanted to use "Clavey" as a constant reminder of the gratitude that we should all have when coexisting with nature.[147]

Today, Clavey Vineyards and Winery is run by Marc's son, Josh Orman, and his family. Josh has been passionate about the winemaking process since he was fifteen years old, and he pursued a degree in enology and viticulture at California Polytechnic State University. While he was in college, Josh received training as an apprentice to master winemaker Duccio Meazzini, the cellar master at Fattoria Lavacchio Vineyard and Winery in Pontassieve, a commune in the Province of Florence in the Italian region of Tuscany. In Italy, Josh learned how to refine his techniques using Old-World traditions. This tradition connected him back to his family's Italian roots.[148] Visitors can taste Clavey wines in their downtown Nevada City tasting room.

Clavey Vineyards. *Courtesy of Clavey Vineyards.*

OUR FUTURE LOOKS BRIGHT

Currently, there are hundreds of acres' worth of grapes growing in local Nevada County vineyards. World-class, highly regarded and awarded wines are now being produced by thirteen wineries in Nevada County. Rumor has it that more wineries will open in the near future. Visitors could spend a long weekend—or even a week—traveling to each winery, meeting the owners and the winemakers personally and having experiences that some say is reminiscent of the way Napa Valley was thirty or forty years ago.

CULTURAL DISTRICT DESIGNATION

In 2018, the California Arts Council selected fourteen districts to serve as California's inaugural state-designated cultural districts. Nevada County is blessed to have two of these fourteen districts: the Grass Valley and Nevada City cultural district and the Truckee cultural district. The California Arts Council defines a cultural district in this way: "A cultural district is a well-defined geographic area with a high concentration of cultural resources and activities."[149] What makes a successful California cultural district? Cultural districts are destinations that are doing well economically and undergoing revitalization. They are also areas that have many artists, arts organizations, activities and attractions. A successful California cultural district is a destination that has an economic influx and revitalization, good retention of artists and arts organizations, retention of homegrown assets and uses and inclusive development.[150]

In addition to Nevada County's active arts cultures, Grass Valley and Nevada City are also known for their expanding vineyards, wineries and tasting rooms and their exceptionally beautiful trail networks. The Grass Valley and Nevada City cultural district is home to the Nevada Theatre, the oldest theater in California, and it has over one hundred arts-related organizations that collectively produce more than one thousand events a year. Some of the area's popular events include annual music festivals, home and garden tours, art studio tours, street fairs and concerts that feature different genres of music. The business districts of Nevada City and Grass Valley, along with their Victorian neighborhoods, grew out of their mining heritage. Today, the historical treasures in these towns have been preserved within each of their main streets, and they have become popular tourist destinations.

Nevada County has a rich history that has been woven through and around its wonderful local wineries and vineyards. These things make Nevada County a truly unique and special place to visit and reside in. Nevada County is proud of its rich artistic community and culture, beauty and quality of life. The area's scenic natural resources, including the South Yuba River and the numerous lakes in the area, make Nevada County a very desirable place to be. Nevada City native and former mayor Bob Paine put it best when he said, "Nevada City's future was in the preservation of its past."

Directory

HISTORIC LOCATIONS

Empire Mine State Park
10791 East Empire Street
Grass Valley, CA
530-273-8522
www.empiremine.org
There is a moderate admission charge to enter the park. There is also a
nice gift shop that helps keep this beautiful California state treasure open
and maintained.

The Firehouse Museum
214 Main Street
Nevada City, CA
530-265-5468
www.nevadacountryhistory.org
This museum displays artifacts from the Nisenan and early pioneer days.

The Kohler Building
15454 Washington Road Washington, CA

The Miners Foundry Cultural Center
325 Spring Street
Nevada City, CA
530-265-5040
www.minersfoundry.org
This historical foundry has a self-guided tour and is available for events
and weddings.

Nevada County Narrow Gauge Railroad Museum
5 Kidder Court
Nevada City, CA
530-470-0902
www.ncngrrmuseum.org
This is an excellent museum of transportation history in Nevada County. It has a wonderful collection of railroad and aviation artifacts, photos and documents and some actual railcars and locomotives.

Nevada Theatre
401 Broad Street Nevada City, CA

The North Star House
12075 Auburn Road
Grass Valley, CA
530-477-7126
www.thenorthstarhouse.org
The public is invited to tour the North Star House and take in the history of this beautiful home.

The North Star Mine Powerhouse and Pelton Wheel Museum
933 Allison Ranch Road
Grass Valley, CA
530-273-4255
www.nevadacountyhistory.org
This museum's exhibits include a replica of an assay room, a blacksmith shop, a dynamite-packing machine and a stamp mill. If you take a guided tour, you might get to see the thirty-foot-tall Pelton Wheel operate. There is as much to see outside the museum as inside, and each piece of equipment is nicely identified if you should choose to take a self-guided tour.

Wells Fargo Express
Pleasant Valley Road and Broad Street French Corral, CA

Wells Fargo & Company
29349 State Route 49 North San Juan, CA

WINERIES

Avanguardia Winery
13028 Jones Bar Road
Nevada City, CA

TASTING ROOM:
163 Mill Street
Grass Valley, CA
530-274-9911
www.avanguardiawines.com
Visit this winery by appointment.

Clavey Vineyards and Winery
TASTING ROOM:
232 Commercial Street
Nevada City, CA
530-265-8200
www.claveywinc.com

Double Oak Vineyards and Winery
14510 Blind Shady Road
Nevada City, CA
530-292-3235
www.doubleoakwinery.com

Gray Pine Vineyard and Winery
19396 Branding Iron Road
Penn Valley, CA
530-432-7045
www.graypinewinery.com.

Lucchesi Vineyards and Winery
VINEYARD:
19698 View Forever Lane
Grass Valley, CA

TASTING ROOM:
128 Mill Street
Grass Valley, CA
530-273-1596
www.lucchesivineyards.com.

Montoliva Vineyard and Winery
15629 Mt. Olive Road
Chicago Park, CA
530-346-6577
www.montoliva.com

Naggiar Vineyards and Tasting Room
18125 Rosemary Lane
Grass Valley, CA
530-268-9059
www.naggiarvineyards.com.

Nevada City Winery
321 Spring Street
Nevada City, CA
530-265-WINE (530-265-9463)
www.ncwinery.com

Nevada County Wine Guild
Pilot Peak Vineyard and Winery
12888 Spenceville Road
Penn Valley, CA
530-432-3321
www.pilotpeak.com.
This winery has no local tasting room to visit, but you can find their wine in stores nationwide or on their website www.ourdailywines.com.

Sierra Starr Vineyard and Winery
VINEYARD AND WINERY:
11179 Gibson Drive
Grass Valley, CA

TASTING ROOM:
124 West Main Street
Grass Valley, CA
530-477-8282
www.sierrastarr.com.
Visit this winery by appointment.

Szabo Vineyards
TASTING ROOM:
316 Broad Street
Nevada City, CA

VINEYARD AND WINERY:
14293 Gold Fork Road
Nevada City, CA
530-265-8792
www.szabovineyards.com
Visit this winery by appointment.

Truckee River Winery
11467 Brockway Road
Truckee, CA
530-587-4626
www.truckeeriverwinery.com.

Notes

Chapter 1

1. Natividad, "Nevada County's Founding Farms and Ranches Laid the Community's Foundation."
2. Dietrich, "Penn Valley, Like No Place on Earth."
3. Mark Winkler, "Penn Valley: Sometimes Corn Is the Gold You're After," Nevada County Gold, www.nevadacountygold.com.
4. Robert Wyckoff, *Nevada County Memories: Presented by the Union Newspaper* (Battle Ground, WA: Pediment Publishing, 2001), 68.
5. "Truckee History and Walking Map," Truckee Chamber of Commerce.
6. "Old Jail Museum," Truckee-Donner Historical Society.

Chapter 2

7. United States Department of Agriculture, *Global Wine Report*, 7–9.
8. Stevenson. *The Sotheby's Wine Encyclopedia*, 462.
9. Borg, "A Short History of Wine Making in California."
10. Ibid.
11. Phylloxera is a pest for commercial grapevines and are almost microscopic, pale yellow, sap-sucking insects. They are related to aphids and feed on the roots and leaves of grapevines. They can be quite destructive.
12. Byers, "Gold Dust, Red Dirt."
13. Ibid.

14. Byers, "A Tip of the Hat to Our Roots."
15. Ibid.
16. Ibid.
17. Ibid.
18. Borg, "A Short History of Wine Making in California."
19. Ibid.

Chapter 3

20. Wilson and Thowne, "Nisenan," in *Handbook of North American Indians*.
21. Ibid.
22. "The Gold Rush Impact on Native Tribes," Public Broadcasting Company (PBS), www.pbs.org.
23. Pritzker, *A Native American Encyclopedia*, 132.
24. Schueller and White, "The California Tribe the Government Tried to Erase in the '60s."

Chapter 4

25. George Knight is the name on the historical marker that commemorates this discovery; however, he is referred to as McKnight in other documents.
26. "More Tales from the Mines," Oakland Museum of California.
27. Brown and Selverston, "Malakoff Diggins," 16–9.
28. "Welcome to the Friends of North Bloomfield and Malakoff Diggins," Malakoff Diggins State Historic Park, www.malakoffdigginsstatepark.org.
29. "Malakoff Diggins State Park," Nevada County Gold, www.ncgold.com.
30. "Gold Country," Nevada City Chamber of Commerce.
31. "Nevada County History," Nevada County Museum.
32. "California Historical Landmarks in Nevada County," NoeHill Travels in California.
33. Ibid.
34. "Kohler Building." NoeHill Travels in California.
35. Cottrell, "Vision Comes to Fruition," *Nevada City Advocate*.
36. Ibid.
37. Ibid.
38. Ibid.
39. Noy, "Area Couple Fought for Women's Rights," *Union Newspaper*.

Chapter 5

40. "Gold Country."
41. "Empire Mine State Historic Park," California Department of Parks and Recreation, www.parks.ca.gov.
42. Ibid.
43. "Discover Gold, Grit and Glory," Empire Mine Association.
44. "The Empire's Success," California Department of Parks and Recreation.
45. Orlo Steele, personal interview for *Golden Stories of Our Past: Forgotten Places* (Nevada County: *The Union Newspaper* Production, 2015).
46. McQuiston Jr., *Gold*.
47. "Discover Gold, Grit and Glory."
48. "History of the North Star House," North Star House, www.thenorthstarhouse.org.
49. Ibid.
50. "North Star Mine Powerhouse and Pelton Wheel Museum," Nevada County Historical Society, www.nevadacountyhistory.org.
51. "Restoring Glory to California Gold Mining," Idaho-Maryland Mine History, Rise Gold Corporation, www.risegoldcorp.com.

Chapter 6

52. Matthew Renda, "Gold Rush Railway."
53. Charles Easton Spooner, *Narrow Gauge Railways*, 1879, 71.
54. Nordell, "Nevada County Narrow-Gauge Railroad (1874–1942)."
55. Wyckoff, *Never Come, Never Go!*
56. *New York Times*, "Heard About Town," March 16, 1899.
57. Bommersback, "Railroad's First Lady," *True West Magazine*.
58. "Home," Nevada County Narrow Gauge Railroad Museum.
59. Browne, *Nuggets of Nevada County History*, 83.
60. Bommersback, "Railroad's First Lady."
61. Nevada County Narrow Gauge Railroad Museum, "Home."
62. Wyckoff, *Never Come, Never Go!*
63. Nordell, "Nevada County Narrow-Gauge Railroad (1874–1942)."
64. Ibid.
65. "Bridgeport History," South Yuba River Park Association.
66. "South Yuba River State Park," Nevada County Gold, www.ncgold.com.

Chapter 7

67. Byers, "A Tip of the Hat to Our Roots," Nevada City Chamber of Commerce.
68. Bean, *History and Directory of Nevada County*, 43–5.
69. Ibid.
70. Ken Zinns, "Old Vine Zinfandel in the Sierra Foothills," www.westcoastwine.net.
71. Bean, *History and Directory of Nevada County*, 43–5.
72. Ibid.
73. Byers, "Gold Dust, Red Dirt."
74. Bean, *History and Directory of Nevada County*, 43–5.
75. Byers, "Gold Dust, Red Dirt."
76. Hamm, *Shaping the Eighteenth Amendment*, 228.
77. Ibid.
78. Byers, "Gold Dust, Red Dirt."
79. Gordon Richards, "Speakeasies Were Truckee's Answer to Prohibition," *Sierra Sun Newspaper*, May 29, 2006.
80. Byers, "Gold Dust, Red Dirt."

Chapter 8

81. Browne, *Nuggets of Nevada County History*, 31–3.
82. "Felix Gillet Biography," Felix Gillet Institute.
83. Parsons, "Felix Gillet," *Nevada County Historical Society Bulletin*.
84. "Felix Gillet Biography," Felix Gillet Institute.
85. Parsons, "Felix Gillet."
86. "Felix Gillet Biography," Felix Gillet Institute.
87. Dickey, "Bierwagen."
88. Ibid.
89. Ibid.
90. Bland, "To Grow Sweeter Produce, California Farmers Turn Off the Water."
91. Byers, "California Grape Vines: Surviving or Thriving?" *Union Newspaper*.
92. Bland, "Field Guide to Sustainable and Delicious Dry-Farmed Wines," *San Francisco Weekly*.
93. Jackson Starr, May 1, 2019, author's conversation via email regarding dry farming.

94. "Dry Farming," California Ag Water Stewardship Initiative (CAWSI).
95. "Dry Farming in California" Community Alliance with Family Farmers.
96. Mary Beth Quirk, "Dry Farming Challenging Everything your Science Teacher Told you, but it Actually Works," NPR, August 28, 2013.
97. Byers, "California Grape Vines."
98. CAWSI, "Dry Farming."
99. Bland, "Field Guide to Sustainable and Delicious Dry-Farmed Wines," *San Francisco Weekly*.
100. Bland, "To Grow Sweeter Produce, California Farmers Turn Off the Water."
101. "The Vineyard Year," Sierra Wine and Grape Growers Association.
102. Cindy Fake, "Growing Grapes in Placer and Nevada Counties," Nevada and Placer Counties.
103. Wine and Spirits Education Trust. *Wine and Spirits: Understanding Wine Quality*, 2–5.

Chapter 9

104. Rod Byers, "Wine by the Numbers: A Look at the Industry in Nevada County," *Union Newspaper*, August 31, 2004.
105. Ibid.
106. Byers, "Gold Dust, Red Dirt."
107. "Wine Regions: The Sierra Foothills," Everyvine, www.everyvine.com.
108. Barbara Keck, *Wineries of the Sierra Foothills*, 64.

Chapter 10

109. "Home," Avanguardia Winery, www.avanguardiawines.com.
110. Marilyn Chrisman, "Conversations about Avanguardia," January 20, 2019.
111. "Lucchesi Vineyards," Nevada County, California, www.gonevadacounty.com.
112. Mario Clough, "Conversations about Lucchesi," January 25, 2019.
113. "Home," Lucchesi Vineyards and Winery, www.lucchesivineyards.com.
114. "Home," Gray Pine Vineyard and Winery, www.graypinewinery.com.
115. Byers, "Gray Pine Vineyard and Winery."

116. Galvan-Davis, Columb, and Columb, "The Peak Partnership," *Destination Nevada County*: 154.

117. "Home," Pilot Peak Winery, www.pilotpeak.com.

118. Ibid.

119. "Pilot Peak Vineyard and Winery," Nevada County, California, www.gonevadacounty.com.

120. "Home," Nevada County Wine Guild, www.ourdailywines.com.

121. Dunne, "Dunne on Wine."

122. "Home," Sierra Starr Vineyard and Winery, www.sierrastarr.com.

123. Ibid.

124. Jackson Starr, "Conversations with Jackson Starr," May 1, 2019.

125. Dunne, "Dunne on Wine."

126. "Home," Szabo Vineyards, www.szabovineyards.com.

127. Ibid.

128. Erin Thiem, "More Nevada City Wine Tasting," Outside Inn Blog, www.outsideinn.com.

129. Susan Phillips, "Meet a Farmer: Mike Naggiar of Naggiar Vineyards," California Grown Blog, March 24, 2017, www.californiagrown.org.

130. "Home," Naggiar Vineyards, www.naggiarvineyards.com.

131. Ibid.

132. "Home," Montoliva Vineyard and Winery, www.montoliva.com.

133. Rod Byers, "The Vine's the Thing," *Union Newspaper*, April 5, 2016, www.theunion.com.

134. Ibid.

135. Montoliva Vineyard and Winery, "Home."

136. Mark Henry, "Author's Conversations with Mark Henry at Montoliva," April 9, 2019.

137. Ibid.

138. Keck, *Wineries of the Sierra Foothills*, 69–71.

139. "Home," Double Oak Vineyards and Winery, www.doubleoakwinery.com.

140. Ibid.

141. "The Oldest Winery in Nevada County, California," Nevada City Winery.

142. Ibid.

143. Ibid.

144. "Highest and Coldest and Snowiest," Truckee River Winery.

145. Ibid.

146. "Home," Clavey Vineyards and Winery, www.claveywine.com.

147. Ibid.

148. Ibid.

149. "Grass Valley: Nevada City Cultural District," California Cultural Districts, www.caculturaldistricts.org.

150. "Welcome to Nevada County Arts Council," Nevada County Arts Council.

Bibliography

Avanguardia Winery. "Welcome to Avanguardia Wines." www. avanguardiawines.com.

Bean, Edwin F. *History and Directory of Nevada County*. Nevada, CA: Printed at the *Daily Gazette* Book and Job Office, 1867, 43–45.

Bland, Alastair. "Field Guide to Sustainable and Delicious Dry-Farmed Wines." *San Francisco Weekly*, June 6, 2011. www.sfweekly.com.

———. "To Grow Sweeter Produce, California Farmers Turn Off the Water." NPR, August 28, 2013. www.npr.org.

Bommersback, Jana. "Railroad's First Lady." *True West Magazine*, March 1, 2007. www.truewestmagazine.com.

Borg, Axel. "A Short History on Wine Making in California." UC Davis Library. www.library.ucdavis.edu.

Brands, H.W. *The Age of Gold: The California Gold Rush and the New American Dream*. New York: Anchor, 2003, 103–121.

Brown, Syd, and Mark Selverston. "Malakoff Diggins." *Destination Nevada County California* (Fall/Winter 2019): 16–19.

Browne, Juanita Kennedy. *Nuggets of Nevada County History*. Nevada, CA: Nevada County Historical Society, 1983.

Byers, Rod. "California Grape Vines, Surviving or Thriving?" *Union Newspaper*, June 4, 2015. www.theunion.com

———. "Gold Dust, Red Dirt: Nevada County's Wine Industry Has a Storied Past." *Union Newspaper*, January 2005.

———. "Gray Pine Vineyard and Winery: Where Cab Is King." *Union Newspaper*, December 3, 2014. www.theunion.com.

———. "A Tip of the Hat to Our Roots." Nevada City Chamber of Commerce. www.nevadacitychamber.com.

———. "The Vine's the Thing." *Union Newspaper*, April 5, 2016. www.theunion.com.

California Cultural Districts. "About the Grass Valley–Nevada City Cultural District." Grass Valley–Nevada City Cultural District. www.caculturaldistricts.org.

California Department of Parks and Recreation. "The Empire's Success." www.parks.ca.gov.

California State Parks. "Park Info." Empire Mine State Historic Park. www.parks.ca.gov.

CAWSI California Ag Water Stewardship Initiative. "Dry Farming." www.agwaterstewards.org.

Clavey Vineyards and Winery. "Home." www.claveywine.com.

Community Alliance with Family Farmers. "Dry Farming in California: Saving Water, Making Great Wine." Dry Farming. www.caff.org.

Cottrell, Steve. "Vision Comes to Fruition." *Nevada City Advocate*, August 2013.

Danielson, Caroline. "Men: Women in Early San Francisco." FoundSF. August 26, 2016. www.foundsf.org.

Dickey, John. "Bierwagen: From Russia to Chicago Park." *Union Newspaper*, July 15, 2002. www.theunion.com.

Dietrich, Teresa. "Penn Valley, Like No Place on Earth." *Destination Nevada County California* (Fall/Winter 2019): 84–85.

Double Oak Vineyards and Winery. "Sierra Mountain Grown Fine Wine." www.doubleoakwinery.com.

Dunne, Michael. "Dunne on Wine: Hatching New Sauvignon Blanc at Sierra Starr Vineyards and Winery." *Sacramento Bee*, July 3, 2017. www.sacbee.com.

Empire Mine Park Association. "Discover Gold, Grit and Glory." www.empiremine.org.

Fake, Cindy. "Growing Grapes in Placer & Nevada Counties." Horticulture and Small Farms Advisor, Nevada and Placer Counties. www.ucanr.edu.

Felix Gillet Institute. "Felix Gillet Biography." About Felix Gillet. www.felixgillet.org.

Galvan-Davis, Robin, Mike Columb and Vanessa Columb. "The Peak Partnership." *Destination Nevada County* 5 (2019): 154.

Gibson, Amber. "Firsts in American Wine." Wine Folly. www.winefolly.com.

Go Nevada County. "Firehouse No. 1 Museum." Nevada City History Museums. www.gonevadacounty.com.

———. "History." www.gonevadacounty.com.

Gray Pine Vineyard and Winery. "Gray Pine Winery." www.graypinewinery.com.

Hamm, Richard F. *Shaping the Eighteenth Amendment: Temperance Reform, Legal Culture, and the Polity, 1880–1920.* Chapel Hill, NC: UNC Press Books, 1995, 228.

History of Nevada County, California. Thompson & West 1880. Howell North Books, Berkeley, CA, 1880.

Jackson, Donald C. *Great American Bridges and Dams.* Hoboken, NJ: Wiley, 1988.

Kaiser, Marge. "The History of Camp Augusta." Camp Augusta Brochure. www.campaugusta.org.

Keck, Barbara. *Wineries of the Sierra Foothills.* Tahoe City, CA: Range of Light Media Group, 2016, 64, 69–71.

Lindstadt, Marlene. "The Kneebone Family History as Related to Bridgeport." Penn Valley Area Chamber of Commerce. www.pennvalleycoc.org.

Lucchesi Vineyards and Winery. "Welcome to Lucchesi Vineyards and Winery." www.lucchesivineyards.com.

Malakoff Diggins State Historic Park. "Friends of North Bloomfield and Malakoff Diggins." www.malakoffdigginsstatepark.org.

McQuiston, F.W., Jr. *Gold: The Saga of the Empire Mine 1850–1956.* Nevada City, CA: Blue Dolphin Press, 1986.

Miners Foundry Cultural Center. "History of Miners Foundry." www.minersfoundry.org.

Montoliva Vineyard and Winery. "Montoliva Vineyard and Winery." www.montoliva.com.

Naggiar Vineyards. "Visit Naggiar." www.naggiarvineyards.com.

Natividad, Ivan. "Nevada County's Founding Farms and Ranches Laid the Community's Foundation." *Union Newspaper*, December 5, 2014.

Nevada City Chamber of Commerce. "Gold Country." History Page, Gold Mining. www.nevadacitychamber.com.

Nevada City Winery. "The Oldest Winery in Nevada County, California." www.ncwinery.com.

Nevada County Arts Council. "Welcome to Nevada County Arts Council." Cultural Districts. www.nevadacountyarts.org.

Nevada County Historical Society. "North Star Mine Powerhouse and Pelton Wheel Exhibit." www.nevadacountyhistory.org.

Nevada County Museum. "Nevada County History." About Nevada County. www.aboutnevadacounty.com.

Nevada County Narrow Gauge Railroad Museum. "Home." www.ncngrrmuseum.org.

Nevada County Wine Guild. "Home." Our Daily Wines. www.ourdailywines.com.

New York Times. "Heard About Town." March 16, 1899.

NoeHill Travels in California. "Kohler Building." California Historical Landmarks in Nevada County. www.noehill.com.

———. "Nevada County California." California Historical Landmarks in Nevada County. www.noehill.com.

Nordell, G.E. "Nevada County Narrow-Gauge Railroad (1874–1942)." G.E. Nordell's California Railroads Pages. www.genordell.com.

Noy, Gary. "Area Couple Fought for Women's Rights; Sen. Aaron Sargent Wrote Words that Became Nineteenth Amendment to U.S. Constitution." *Union Newspaper*, June 17, 2004.

Oakland Museum of California. "More Tales from the Mines." www.explore.museumca.org.

Parsons, C.E. "Felix Gillet." *Nevada County Historical Society Bulletin* 16, no. 4, (November 1962).

Pilot Peak Winery. "Pilot Peak Winery: It's the Wine—the People—the Place." www.pilotpeak.com.

Pritzker, Barry M. *A Native American Encyclopedia: History, Culture, and Peoples.* Oxford, UK: Oxford University Press, 2000, 132.

Remolif, Sandra. "Malakoff Diggins State Park." Nevada County Gold. www.ncgold.com.

Renda, Matthew. "Golden Past: How Mining Shaped Western Nevada County." *Union Newspaper*, April 25, 2014.

———. "Gold Rush Railway: Nevada County Narrow Gauge Railroad Provided Faster Track for Community, Gold-Mining Industry." *The Union Newspaper*, May 27, 2014.

Richards, Gordon. "Speakeasies Were Truckee's Answer to Prohibition." *Sierra Sun Newspaper*, May 29, 2006. www.sierrasun.com.

Rise Gold Corporation. "Restoring Glory to California Gold Mining." Idaho-Maryland Mine History. www.risegoldcorp.com.

Schueller, Brooke, and Avery White. "The California Tribe the Government Tried to Erase in the '60s." *VICE Media*, January 16, 2018.

Sierra Nevada Geotourism. "Site of One of the First Discoveries of Quartz Gold in California." Historic Site or District. www.sierranevadageotourism. com.

Sierra Starr Vineyard and Winery. "Welcome to Sierra Starr." www. sierrastarr.com.

Sierra State Parks Foundation. "History and Mountain Lake Fun Await You." Donner Memorial State Park. www.sierrastateparks.org.

Sierra Wine and Grape Growers Association. "The Vineyard Year." www. swgga.org.

South Yuba River State Park Association. "Bridgeport History." www. southyubariverstatepark.org.

———. "Welcome to the South Yuba River State Park Association." www. southyubariverstatepark.org.

Stevenson, Tom. *The Sotheby's Wine Encyclopedia*. 4th ed. London: Dorling Kindersly, 2005.

Szabo Vineyards. "Szabo Vineyards." www.szabovineyards.com.

Thiem, Erin. "South Yuba River State Park." Nevada County Gold. www. ncgold.com.

Truckee Chamber of Commerce. "Truckee Cultural District." www. chamber.truckee.com.

———. "Truckee History and Walking Map." Truckee History. www.truckee. com.

Truckee-Donner Historical Society. "Old Jail Museum." Historical Assets. www.truckeehistory.org.

Truckee River Winery. "Highest and Coldest and Snowiest." www. truckeeriverwinery.com.

United States Department of Agriculture. *Global Wine Report*. August 2006, 7–9.

Wilson, Norman L., and Arlean H. Thowne. "Nisenan." In *Handbook of North American Indians*. Edited by William C. Sturtevant. Washington, D.C.: Smithsonian Institution, 1987.

Wine and Spirits Education Trust. *Wine and Spirits: Understanding Wine Quality*. 2nd revised ed. London: Wine and Spirits Education Trust, 2012, 2–5.

Winkler, Mark. "Penn Valley History." Nevada County Gold. www. nevadacountygold.com.

Wyckoff, Robert M. "Nevada County Memories." *The Union Newspaper*, 2001.

———. *Never Come, Never Go! The Story of Nevada County's Narrow Gauge Railroad*. Nevada City, CA: Nevada City Publishing Company, 1986.

Index